Affirm press

Fiona Scott-Norman is a Melbourne-based writer, performer, director and broadcaster. She writes for *The Big Issue* and is a regular on ABC Radio.

EDITED BY

FIONA SCOTT-NORMAN

HARD KNOCKS

Outstanding Australians on
Hard Lessons Learned at High School

Affirm press

Affirm press
books that leave an impression

28 Thistlethwaite Street, South Melbourne,
Boon Wurrung Country, VIC 3205
affirmpress.com.au
10 9 8 7 6 5 4 3 2 1

Title: Hard Knocks/ Fiona Scott-Norman, editor
ISBN: 9781922626875 (paperback)

NATIONAL LIBRARY OF AUSTRALIA
A catalogue record for this book is available from the National Library of Australia

Photo of Christos Tsiolkas by Zoe Ali
Photo of Benjamin Law by Daniel Francisco Robels
Photo of Annie Louey by Nick Walters
Photo of Missy Higgins by Cybele Malinowski

Cover design by Karen Wallis, Taloula Press
Typeset in Garamond Premier Pro by J&M Typesetting
Proudly printed in Australia by Griffin Press

FSC www.fsc.org MIX Paper from responsible sources FSC® C009448

The paper this book is printed on is certified against the Forest Stewardship Council® Standards. Griffin Press holds chain of custody certification SGSHK-COC-005088. FSC® promotes environmentally responsible, socially beneficial and economically viable management of the world's forests.

CONTENTS

INTRODUCTION

When people find out I was unpopular at high school – and I was weapons-grade unpopular – they pull a sympathetic face. They lean in, touch my arm and say, 'Of *course* – you're a redhead.' And I'm like, 'Ah, no. I colour my hair. I was bullied because of my personality.'

And we laugh because it's a good joke. But it's also true. I was white, smart and readerly at a middle-class boarding school in England, at a time where white, smart and readerly were essentially the entry requirements. And yet, as Yoda would say, fit in, I did not. For years I was the most excluded student out of a cohort of two thousand.

Why me? To misquote Jane Austen, 'It is a truth universally acknowledged, that a school in possession of a homogenous student population, must be in want of a scapegoat.' The schoolyard is a hierarchy: someone has to be at the bottom of the pecking order, and it's usually the kid who's most obviously different.

I was ill-prepared for boarding school at eleven. I was precocious and clueless on how to behave around kids my age (only child, adopted, much older parents, moved around a lot, friends were mostly books). At primary school, I was 'no-mates McGee' and spent lunchtimes playing chess with, bless his heart, my form teacher. I was super tall, short-sighted and gangly (Marfan syndrome), and also hypersensitive and flinchy (shouty dad). Also, I was not sporty, thank you for asking.

At high school I was visible in an unwelcome way, notoriously 'other', and was pointed out to new students during their orientation: 'There's the hockey field, that's the main dining room – avoid the mashed potato, it's always lumpy – and over there, that tall, hunched skinny girl with knock-knees, glasses and neediness you can see from Jupiter? That's Spider.'

Great nickname for a little girl – sigh. And once a nickname's stuck, unless you can rock it, you're dead meat. I did not rock it. I was very, *very* lonely, made jokes to pretend I didn't care, buried myself in books and cartoon strips, and batted myself like a moth against the closed window of acceptance.

But that's schools for you. They're all chockers with schoolkids desperate to fit in because, evolutionarily, social exclusion led to, well, death. Way back, being cast out by your community meant no access to food, fire or support, so we are wired to experience sheer existential terror if we don't belong. School can be brutal, as we instinctually do What It Takes to stay close to the warmth of that metaphoric fire: suppress the bits of ourselves that are deemed unacceptable, suck up to the popular group, shun anyone on the fringes.

Australian government research suggests that the proportion of students affected by bullying, whether it's cyberbullying or IRL, hovers at around one in four. A quarter of every school is a lot of kids not fitting in and suffering for it. I doubt 25 per cent would even touch the sides of who's having a terrible time, because stacks of 'just fine, thanks' kids are hiding who they really are and scared numb they'll be found out. Bit of a secret: it's not just you. School is frequently, genuinely, quite shit. It is categorically *not* the best days of your life.

Hard Knocks is a collection of interviews with 22 of the most intriguing, talented, accomplished and admired people in Australia. They're leading big, creative, courageous lives, shining bright, pulling others up behind them. And for all of them, their school years were dark and hard; they were misfits bullied from pillar to post, reviled, rejected or judged, unable or unwilling to fit the only box they were being offered. Adam Goodes, Alice Pung, Annie Louey, Benjamin Law, Brendan Cowell, Carly Findlay, Charlie Pickering, Christos Tsiolkas, Corey Tutt, Eddie Perfect, Holden Sheppard, Hazem El Masri, Judith Lucy, Karen from Finance, Kate Miller-Heidke, Megan Washington, Missy Higgins, Mo'Ju, Paul Capsis, Penny Wong, Stella Young and Tiffiny Hall have all shared the battlegrounds of their school experiences. They are revelatory.

Some of these stories are confronting, others less intense. But the common ground is not just surviving but flourishing despite great obstacles. After school, they all transformed from 'kid most likely to be spat on' into high-achieving, charismatic individuals. This is not a coincidence. Being unique and unaccepted meant having to confront adversity and find ways through, over and past it. They've all been shaped by the fight to be themselves and do things their way. Their stories are blueprints for becoming yourself, offering strategies to cope and conquer and inspiring and inventive ways to deal with the undealwithable. Turns out there's an advantage to not being accepted at school: you are forced to fall back on your own resources.

You may relate most to Corey Tutt – underestimated, taunted

and living with PTSD – who is now making science accessible for a generation of Indigenous students. Or perhaps you'll respond to Tiffiny Hall, who was crippled with shyness; Mo'Ju, who hid in music as they battled with identity issues, racism and exclusion; or Holden Sheppard, who masked his personality and homosexuality, grew up terrified of making a mistake and finally wrote himself into existence.

None of them, with hindsight, wishes away anything. They're who they are because of what they've been through. It's not to suggest that being bullied, or facing any adversity, is desirable or necessary, but there's no question that there are positives that become apparent in retrospect. Being able to get through it and come out the other side gives you strength, self-reliance and confidence in your originality.

Many years after finishing school and moving to Australia, where I became a writer, arts journalist, DJ, broadcaster and comedian, I met up with some dorm-mates from school on a trip back to the UK. They were all mothers and, from memory, physiotherapists, which is perfectly valid, but I saw where my life would have gone if I'd fitted in and not forged my own path and I realised I'd escaped.

There's no shame in being bullied or not fitting in. It's inevitable that if you're unique, 'other' in some way, school will not be easy. The more unusual someone is, the more hard knocks there will be, but once you leave school, the individuality that was the albatross around your neck becomes a highly prized and sought-after commodity. There are long-term benefits to being forced to be your own person; no one becomes great by fitting in or just disappearing.

And although school, due to a little-known clause in Einstein's theory of relativity, feels like it lasts forever, it's an illusion. Before you know it, school will be in your rear-view mirror so fast you'll have to squint to see it as you speed towards your actual life.

Content warning: *Hard Knocks* is intended as the safest of spaces, so I will flag that there's *content* within these pages – the kind that often requires a warning. But if you're holding this book, you're anticipating references to bullying, mental-health issues and hardship. Much as you'd expect a jar of peanut butter to contain traces of nuts.

The purpose of *Hard Knocks* is to show that if you're suffering, you're *not* alone. Whatever you're experiencing, others have been there, and it has made them what they are. Obstacles are often the flipside of becoming exceptional.

This is less a warning, then, and more of a welcome. The extraordinary Australians in *Hard Knocks* have known bullying, ostracism, neglect, loneliness, depression, anxiety, suicidal ideation, violence, intergenerational trauma, racism, contempt, cultural pressures, homophobia, persecution, misogyny, poverty and classism. In other words, they're *our* kind of people.

All of the love,
Fiona Scott-Norman

MISSY
HIGGINS

Sensitive, anxious, and uncomfortable with attention, Melissa 'Missy' Morrison Higgins was an unlikely candidate for pop stardom. But despite buckling under depression and self-doubt at school, Missy Higgins has become one of Australia's most cherished singer–songwriters. Her first album, *The Sound of White*, went platinum nine times, and she had three straight number-one albums. Her fifth, *Solastalgia*, named for the distress of climate change, was ARIA nominated, and she regularly contributes to film and television soundtracks. 'Torchlight', for the film *Don't Tell*, won an APRA for Best Original Song Composed for the Screen in 2017, and 'Carry You', for Tim Minchin's series *Upright*, was nominated in 2021.

Having loving parents, a stable home, and two adoring older siblings didn't protect Melbourne-born Missy from a despairing childhood. Emotionally she was a small, battered craft on a turbulent ocean, and the effort required to stay even-keeled led to recreational drug use and a dramatic implosion in Year 11.

Songwriting became her coping mechanism. At boarding school she hid away with a piano, pouring her pain and alienation into the alchemy of composition. At 15, a school music assignment prompted a song, 'All for Believing', dedicated to her then-boyfriend. Missy's sister secretly entered it into Triple J Unearthed; it won, and Missy was signed before she left school.

Today Missy Higgins is a nine-time ARIA award winner, renowned for her transformative, poignant ballads. The vulnerability that plagued her at school is now her greatest asset: turning 'feeling too much' into art is Missy Higgins' career, and she's found a safe space in performing.

I was a freak, basically. I was always a deep thinker as a kid. I'd baffle my parents with questions like, 'Why are we here?' and 'What is the meaning of life?' I always had this instinctive feeling that I was from another planet, that I was cut from a different cloth. For years and years I wrote in my diary: *Why am I so different? Why does nobody understand me?* Oh, and lots of esoteric poetry. I never felt the same as anyone else, and I thought that would be it, forever. My problems, really, were mostly internally generated.

It's weird, because until I was six, I was extroverted. I'm the youngest, so I got all the attention, my family loved me, and I was a happy little outgoing kid. And then something happened, I don't know what, and I suddenly became self-conscious, sensitive, aware of myself. My parents said they noticed this sadness, a melancholia, descending on me when I was six or seven. I'd realised that people have opinions, and could be judgemental. I'd realised I needed to be a certain way to be liked. And I *really* wanted to be liked. I couldn't *bear* the thought of someone hating me. So I made myself small. I didn't want to be noticed. That way I wouldn't say anything that might get me laughed at.

I wasn't really bullied in primary school; I just never felt like I fitted in. There were lots of girls from the housing commission. They were rough, tough, wouldn't take shit from anybody, and they scared me. I didn't connect with anyone. I used to come home crying and saying I didn't want to go back.

I was a tomboy, and pretty shy. I was an especially complicated child. Always a bit socially anxious, I attached myself to more confident kids to fit in; I'd find some and follow them around, walk in their shadow. I had this one friend, Victoria, and she was the class clown. I was like the sidekick. I'd whisper things in her ear, and she'd say it out loud and get a huge laugh. I was never a leader or a cool kid. What I did was ... watch. I did a lot of watching. I was very much inside my own head. Looking outwards. Observing.

My parents let me change schools, and when I left in Grade 4, I have the clearest memory of everyone else hugging, and crying, and saying 'I'll see you next year', or 'I'm going to miss you', and I didn't say goodbye to anyone. I just walked out the school gate with my backpack on, and a big smile on my face. I was so happy to see the back of them.

In middle school I was a completely different person. Much more sure of myself. I'm not sure why. Perhaps because there were only five girls in my grade, but it was also a more carefree school. I still had the feeling deep inside that I wasn't like any of them, but it was alright, because I had some friends to laugh with and I was beginning to understand that everyone feels misunderstood.

Then I went to boarding school in Geelong in Year 8. On the one hand I loved it, but again there were some pretty hard-core girls. I was toughening my skin by that stage, but there were a few times I was definitely bullied. There was one girl who'd pick on someone randomly, and put her entire energy into it. She was a powerful girl – sly, secretive, and manipulative – and there was no standing up to her. I got picked on for a while.

She always got someone else to do her evil errands – she had this little 'slave' girl who did everything – and she got her 'slave' to break into my sports locker, and get my undies, which had my nametag on them, and put soy sauce on them so it looked like dried blood. Then she put my undies on the end of a stick, took them around to the Boys' House and showed them off: 'Look! Missy had her period! It's so gross! Look at the blood!'

That burned an indelible image on my mind. It was so harsh; it really threw me. I felt like I'd been betrayed and humiliated for something that was a complete lie. Of course I was far too embarrassed to go to the Boys' House and say, 'It's not true!' It was awful. I just wanted to go home, or stay in bed and never come out again.

For quite a while the boys would snigger when they passed me. Kids love stringing things out when they happen to other people. That feeling of humiliation and betrayal lasted for ages, as it does when you're at school, because it's your entire world, and what other people think of you is so important. Luckily I had a couple of friends who knew what really happened, but you still feel isolated. I put a lot of time into avoiding that girl; I didn't want to be chosen again.

In Year 9, I went to a different boarding school for a year. It was one of those places where parents send their kids if they can't handle them, or they don't want to parent them, or their kids are screwed up, or they come from families that are dysfunctional anyway, or because they have a lot of money. Everyone had intense problems.

In my unit of sixteen girls, there was a cutter, a couple of bulimics, two anorexics, one girl who was constantly suicidal, a couple who were manic depressives, and one girl with chronic fatigue. It was crazy. For probably the first time in my life I felt like the most normal person there. It may have been a blessing in disguise as I realised everyone my age has problems.

It's such an intense age as a girl, fourteen, fifteen, because you've just got your period and your hormones are off the charts. You're all over the place. All this stuff is happening to your body, emotions, and mind, and *none* of it makes sense. To be at boarding school, sleeping in a small building with sixteen girls who didn't know what the hell they were doing either, was like being in a pressure cooker. The tumultuous friendships! The fights! The drama! There was nothing to hold on to, because the likelihood of your friends going through something serious and destabilising was very high.

I was struggling with my own issues – with happiness a lot of the time – and I remember it being hard. I had a fever one night, and a night terror. I woke up and started screaming, waking everyone. I've always sleepwalked, but I was jumping around the room like a monkey and banging my head on the floor, pointing at my best friend and screaming, 'You don't understand! It's coming! It's coming for her!' I could see this black heaviness descending on her, and it was consuming everything in its path. It was my fault somehow, and she didn't know, only I knew, and no one understood. That's a reflection of how intense things were. Now it feels like a metaphor for depression.

This is when I discovered songwriting. There was a little room with a piano in it next to the dormitory. I'd been inspired by music class, where we had to write a song for a project. Composing gave me this flooding sensation, and I knew immediately it was a way to let things go. At this point it was all a bit Celine Dionesque, because that's what I was listening to. I try and pretend that time never existed ...

In Year 10, back in Geelong, I was songwriting in earnest. I'd go and lock myself in the music room, with the piano, for hours and hours and hours – at recess, and lunch, and after school, and on weekends. No one else wanted it on weekends, so I was usually the only one there. I discovered that I could put all my questions about life into my music and lyrics.

There was a comfort in music that I wasn't finding anywhere else, because it was non-judgemental. I'd get a warm feeling, that I was in a place where I was meant to be, where I was accepted. And it was an incredible way to be understood. I could express myself in a way that I couldn't through conversation, the way that normal people did. I ended up performing at every assembly, every school concert, any opportunity; singing this heartfelt stuff to a bunch of kids that I'd never have the guts to say in real life.

My world was completely blown open towards the end of Year 10, when my sister took me out for dinner one school holiday and confessed that she and my brother had been taking party drugs for a few years. My sister and brother were seven and eight years older than me, and I worshipped them. They were going out to clubs every weekend and taking ecstasy, that's what everyone was doing, and I'd had no idea.

I couldn't believe it. Up until then I thought drug addicts lived on the street and killed people. I'd told my sister that a friend and I were considering taking acid, because we'd heard on the grapevine it could be fun, and she told me that if I was going to try drugs, she wanted to be there to oversee it and help control it, and to find the drugs for me. From then on, I was doing it.

It turned out that the guy I was dating, who was a couple of years older than me, was really into ecstasy and partying, and had been high all these times we'd been together. He'd kept it from me, and told my sister not to tell, because he didn't want to expose me to it. But then I started too, and I got right into it. At first it was pretty fun and amazing. I was coming from a headspace where I was always disconnected, and to suddenly feel connected to the people around me *and* the whole world ... It was exactly what I'd been looking for, really.

But it got hugely detrimental. I was sixteen and going out to bars, hanging with my brother and sister and their friends. Fake ID was big currency in those days. You'd buy them off your friends' older sisters. I probably used to look older than I do now, I wore so much make-up, big high heels, short skirts, everything I could do to oblige the bouncer to let me into the club. It's funny, yeah? I feel like I was a completely different person back then.

Going between school, and being out taking drugs with people in their mid-to-late twenties, was a really weird thing to do to my still-developing brain. I just couldn't function after these big weekends. I couldn't ever get my emotions together because I'd be a wreck for the next week or two. It was awful.

I was terrified of all of the new feelings I was having anyway, I was trying to figure out who I was, my place in the world, and I still had that feeling of not being understood. And I was so self-conscious too. Ooh, that was big. I was self-conscious about what everybody thought, what I looked like, and I assumed everyone was being critical. Yeah, so that combined with the effects of the party drugs ... It was just too much.

I haven't been interested in drugs for a long, long time now because the comedown is so severe. They have such a bad effect on my mental health. When I think back it's a creepy feeling actually. There were so many half-blackouts, my vision literally jumping four feet one way then the next, and having complete out-of-body experiences for two seconds at a time. I remember getting into cars with lots of strange men, taking drugs given to me by strange older men. Lots of stupid, stupid things. I was way, way too trusting. I can't believe I survived it.

At the time I dealt with it by getting stuck into studying, because that was the one thing I could control. It became obsessive. I studied and studied and studied. There was so much going on that I didn't understand, and maths problems were something that I could solve. I could tick that box. The teachers clearly had no idea as they even made me a prefect, which is quite ironic.

It would have been hard for anyone else to see what was really going on. My hard time was entirely self-generated. I was a master at keeping all the anxiety in my head. I swallow it in. I've been told I looked really confident, and people even thought of me as one of the cool ones. It certainly never felt like that. I was having a completely different experience to what people saw. I still do that to this day, I think. When I'm struggling I just become very absent. Internal and aloof.

In Year 11, I was a straight A student, and I was not coping. I was manic, stressed, and trying my hardest to not fall apart emotionally. Year 11 is when they really put the pressure on you. All of a sudden it's not enough to be working out who you are, or what so-and-so thinks about you. You have to get good grades and figure out what you're going to do with the rest of your life. So much pressure! It was coming all year, but then I had a collapse. A literal breakdown.

The feeling that I wanted to die, which I often had, had been creeping up and getting louder and louder. Accumulating. Even though I studied hard, I had a lot of trouble with keeping my head above water when it came to schoolwork. I'd get this project done, then this project, then this project, and I managed most of the time. But then close to exams about five or six came in at once, and I thought, 'There's no way I can get all that done. No way.' So I put it off, and then I *didn't* have enough time to do it all, and then it was too much. An overload. It was crushing me, and I didn't know how to manage.

The girls I envied were the ones who seemed to have their shit together. They were incredibly focused, and able to balance sport with social life with studying. I really don't know how they did it. How do you know at that age which direction to go in? How? I felt like I was on a galloping horse without any reins.

In the dining hall one evening, I was looking at my friend sitting opposite, and feeling completely in another world. Everything was spinning, I felt so depressed, overwhelmed, and disassociated from her and everyone in the room. The world was coming in on me really heavily. I'd been trying to keep it at bay for so long, and I couldn't, just couldn't do it anymore.

I wanted to die so badly. I was so resentful that I couldn't just switch myself off. I left the dining hall thinking, 'I can't do this anymore,' and collapsed. I wanted to die or leave my body, so I switched my body off and fell to the ground. I was still conscious, but pretending not to be, because I really, really, didn't want to be.

I remember the sound of people running, and this sweet boy called Andy Hunt picking me up and running with me. At the boarding house the housemaster looked me over, and began shaking me and shouting at me, and it all became very urgent. Then at the hospital they poked and prodded me, and opened my eyelids and shone a torch in. I heard, 'Looks like she hasn't fainted. Her pupils aren't dilated,' and I'm thinking, 'F**k'. And I started crying, and the game was up.

They put me in hospital for a while, and then I went home. I still don't really know what happened. There's depression in my family, but I think the drugs made it into something I couldn't deal with. It's hard to know what's hereditary. I was overwhelmed by the pressures of growing up and not knowing who I was, not ever being as happy and carefree as the other kids. I guess I always felt this weight on me, and I just gave in one day.

It helped in that I had to admit to my parents that I was really struggling. I look back now and can't believe it, but I hadn't told them anything before. Maybe if I had I wouldn't have needed such a big breakdown. But every time I tried to explain, I could never really articulate it. That's why my diary was full of sprawling existential anxiety attacks.

I phoned home on the day, from the hospital, and said, 'Dad, I think I've got depression.' He was quiet on the phone for a bit, and then told me about the depression in his family, and how he's been on antidepressants for a long time. And then he apologised because he said I probably inherited it. But for me, really, it was nice, because for the first time I'd found someone who did understand. It helped a lot. We spoke the same language.

The big relief was that I won Triple J's Unearthed, which got me a record deal, and I was able to relax and enjoy Year 12. I knew I was going to be a musician, which meant I didn't have to try so hard with school. I was able to hang out with my friends and not be strung out about grades and stuff. I was like, 'I'm not going to uni anyway.'

I'm still a sensitive unit, and it's funny, I still don't really want to be noticed. But there's a difference between expressing my feelings through abstract metaphors to an audience of quiet, well-behaved, sitting-down people who I don't have to interact with, and, you know, getting up in front of twenty friends in a room and confessing my deepest feelings. I can never do speeches at parties or weddings, because I get up and my voice starts shaking.

Performing, to me, is much more comfortable than person-to-person interaction, because performing is a controlled space. When I've written a song it expresses a part of me in exactly the way I want to express it, in exactly the way that feels good and right to me, and I don't need to give away any more than I want. It's a controlled way of connecting with people, I guess. It's great.

But plenty of people who are shy as teenagers go on to perform. It's really common. A lot of shy people find it hard to express themselves in other ways, and sometimes you need to have come from that to make good art.

Performing ended up being the way of connecting with people that I was looking for. The ability to turn my struggles into an art form is pretty much my career. If I didn't have any internal struggles going on, and I was able to express myself freely, and life was just a breeze, I'd have no reason to pour myself out into my songs, and I'd have no real subject matter.

And I'd have had no reason to turn to music as a refuge. Music became my channel of expression because I couldn't express myself in any other way. That's why it became such a passion. There's nothing like going through some hard times to come up with creative ways of expressing yourself. I have no doubt it's helped me become the musician and artist that I am today.

Obviously I still struggle with depression occasionally, but I know how to exorcise my demons. And in a way that turns the ugly stuff into something beautiful. That's a great thing. Who knows what would have become of my life if I hadn't gone through all of that and found the necessity of writing it down and turning it into music?

For some reason, when you're a kid, not fitting in is a bad thing. You're not allowed to be an individual at school. The big moment for me was when I realised my differences were actually a positive. Particularly in the creative world, because to do anything worthwhile you've got to think in a way that no one's thought before. To come up with something truly original you've got to be a truly original person.

And not only is it okay to be different, but I've also worked out that I'm not as different as I thought I was. We all have fears and insecurities, and those similarities are ultimately what connect us.

I've also learned how to share. It's hard to be understood if you don't. That was a great learning curve for me. If you've never shared your problems, it feels like it would be humiliating and make matters worse. You don't realise how common what you're going through is. It's even really hard to admit things to your parents; I mean, you want your parents to be proud of you. But when I spoke to my dad I felt a weight lift off me straight away, and I continue to learn how good it is to express and share yourself. It's definitely better in the long run, no matter if it feels counter-intuitive to let your guard down.

These days I'm kind of addicted to it. I'm a confessor. I know if I hold on to things, it's only going to cause me trouble. Obviously you can't do it with everyone, but to talk to someone who will respect and support you can be just life saving.

I reckon that those who struggle in high school are often sensitive, and deep thinkers. And that's a hard thing to be amid a heap of kids who have a more confident personality and a thicker skin. You're gonna get crucified. But it seems you have to struggle and have a complicated brain to come up with these colourful ways of presenting your inner world outwards. It's how artists are made. It's a shame, almost, that it has to be that way, but at least it's turning struggle into something beautiful that the world needs.

Whenever I meet a kid who's in Year 11 or 12, I want to say, 'Don't worry. It really doesn't matter that much.' Unless you want to be a doctor, or lawyer, and you *really* need high grades, in the end it's not the be-all and end-all to get 99 per cent in your VCE exam. It's too much to put on a kid, way too much. The kids who really want it can cope with it, but if you don't, it's a ridiculous pressure.

Once you leave school it's like it was all a dream. When you're there it feels like it's your life, and the school system is built that way too; it's your universe. You think, if you don't fit in here, well, you'll never fit in, and everyone will always be mean to you because you deserve it. You don't have enough life experience yet to realise that it's *their* problem. But, looking back, school is just a holding pen. It's to keep you occupied until you get into the real world – and be free to be whoever you want, and do whatever you want.

ADAM GOODES

Adam Goodes, proud Adnyamathanha and Narungga man, is a legend. Firstly for his former career as a champion AFL player; co-captain of the Sydney Swans, a dual Brownlow medallist and four-time All-Australian. But even more for his emergence as an anti-racist advocate and leader. In 2011 he co-founded the GO Foundation to empower Indigenous role models, and was Australian of the Year in 2014.

In a sport where bad behaviour is often winked at, 'Goodesy' was a beacon of principle. During the Indigenous round in 2013, he pulled up a teenage spectator who called him 'an ape'. The racist backlash led to Adam retiring early. Two 2019 documentaries, *The Final Quarter* and *The Australian Dream*, unpacked his treatment. The AFL offered an unreserved apology.

Adam stood up for himself under unrelenting pressure, and emerged an icon focused on transforming his community. Today the GO Foundation provides scholarships into 27 schools and five universities. A painting of Adam by Vincent Namatjira won the 2020 Archibald Prize, the first Indigenous artist to do so.

Adam's courage and resilience can be traced back to his school years. His mum, Lisa May, moved the family around, and Adam was bounced from school to school, constantly dealing with new faces and, of course, racism. With separated parents, and as the eldest of three boys, he had to grow up fast.

His mum's support was rock solid but it was discovering AFL in high school that saved Adam from going off the rails. Adam credits his footy mates with keeping him on track with schoolwork, protecting him from bullies and teaching him discipline and confidence. Adam still believes in sport but in 2021 he refused induction into the AFL Hall of Fame.

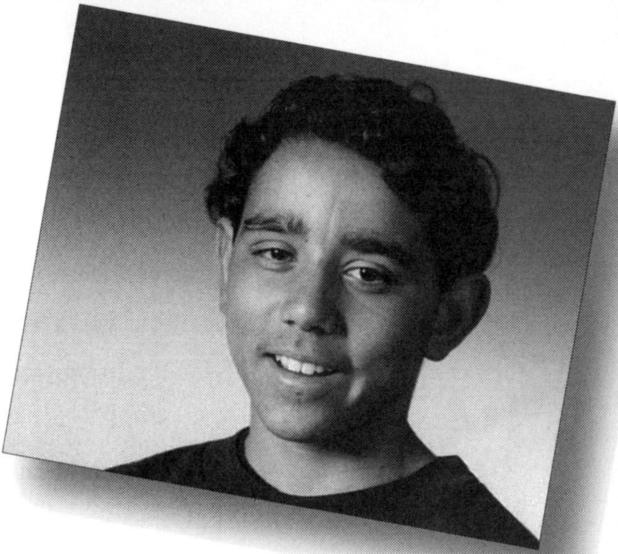

Growing up, I went to about six different primary schools. Going to school was very hard, because we moved quite a bit due to mum being part of the Stolen Generation. We moved closer to family, and away from family, closer to an uncle, or aunty, that mum was keeping in touch with, or one of mum's sisters that she hadn't seen before – because she was taken away when she was five. I couldn't even try to comprehend how hard it was for her.

Mum was looking for family ever since she realised in high school that she had other brothers and sisters she had no idea of. She always wondered who that Indigenous man was that followed her to and from school and it was her father. You know, she really had no relationship with her mum and dad when she was taken away and it's the biggest thing that's affected her. Moving around was a constant thing because she could never feel settled in the one spot.

Mum gave us so much support. She sacrificed a lot to see that we got to school and had food in our tummies. She didn't want us to have the upbringing she had, living in a foster family. I think, in her mind, if she didn't look after her family, the government would take her kids off her, like what had happened to her mum. She didn't want that, and it's a pretty good motivation right there. I can thank her for that, she helped me and my brothers grow into cultured young men. One of my younger brothers now works as a Rock Art Cultural Heritage Protection Specalist at Parks Victoria and my littlest brother is the Manager SA/NT for the Indigenous Defence & Infrastructure Consortium (IDIC).

I was a very shy kid. It was partly because I was born in January, so I was always one of those kids that was a lot younger than everybody else. And I wasn't sure of myself. You know, moving from place to place, meeting a new bunch of kids in class, at every school, having people look at you because you dress funny, because you look different from what they do. I just felt, 'Gee, I don't know if I want to say too much here.' It wasn't until sport that I really started to feel comfortable in my own skin and comfortable in my classes.

Mostly, though, I think it was because I didn't know who I was. I actually had no idea growing up what it meant to be Aboriginal. I remember at one school we got to learn a little bit of Aboriginal language, and that was an awesome experience for me. So special. I always knew I was different from everybody else from the colour of my skin, but it wasn't until I moved to Sydney for football and did a Diploma in Aboriginal Studies, that I realised what it actually meant to be Aboriginal.

It wasn't until high school that I first realised I was, you know ... different. We moved to Horsham in country Victoria, and I think I was one of only two Aboriginal people until my brothers eventually came to high school and picked the numbers up. That's when I got the racism, the bullying from the Year 12s.

It was just stuff like ... people would call me, you know, 'boong', 'coon', 'you black c**t'. Whenever I walked past these particular people I could see them looking at me. They'd sometimes throw things, and would snicker things I couldn't understand, but I could tell that their attention was focused on me, and it wasn't positive energy they were focusing on me. It was very negative.

There was one kid in a year below me who just really wanted to fight me because I was Aboriginal. It didn't eventuate, but he really wanted to beat me up. I wasn't a violent kid. I wasn't an aggressive kid at all, but I was always a big kid, I had a bit of size about me, and I think that sort of protected me from getting the physical bullying, and I was very grateful for that. Most of the stuff I encountered was verbal.

When I was living in Mildura, I had to walk past this one guy's house every day to catch the bus. He would always taunt me at school, and it made me scared to walk past his place, but he'd never say anything when I actually did. I think he wanted to be cool, show me how tough he was in front of his mates.

At Horsham I had racial taunts from one guy in particular, and he would bully not just me, but he'd bully my friends into bullying me. He was very clever. While we were playing sports – footy or softball or whatever – he'd bully them to come and hit me, or he'd hit them. Those sorts of things.

I didn't feel completely isolated, because I had fantastic friends that accepted me, and I think the reason why was sport. It played a vital role for me and my brothers in high school. I had the natural ability to just pick up a ball and hit it, throw it, kick it, whatever, and kids would always want me to be first or second on their team, so at a very junior level, as well, sport was the real driver for me being accepted.

Having moved from place to place, to finally settle in Horsham, it took a while, a couple of weeks into school, before I went out onto the oval. The principal had hooked me up with some people he thought I'd be like, because they were the ones hanging out at the bus shelter and smoking, those sorts of things, and that wasn't really me, so I took it upon myself to be active.

So I went outside and there were these kids kicking the footy, about 60 of them, and I went out there and took one big mark, and suddenly a group of those guys just accepted me. And as soon as footy season came around I signed up with Sunnyside, one of the local AFL sides, and that was my group of mates. All the other guys I'd become friends with were guys that I played footy against, and I think having that base of friends made it easier for me to get through the bullying. I had the benefit of having other people to talk to, other people going through the same situation, so we could talk and just laugh it off. You know, 'Oh what about that loser in Year 12 who always tries to bully us?'

I don't think I would have got through Year 12 without my friends in sport. Sport definitely gave me the confidence to do my homework and ask questions. There were a lot of kids in my situation, playing sport and trying to finish their VCE, and we'd go over to friends' houses and do our footy training, then sit around for two hours afterwards doing our homework. If I'd just gone home, I very much doubt I would have done the work. When there was a big game coming up and I was going to have to miss a day, the teachers would really support me – help me get up to speed so I wouldn't miss too much, and they'd check up on me to make sure I had my assignments done.

I had a lot of joy, you know. I had good friends who went above and beyond for me, and eventually a big family growing up that was really close. In some ways all the moving around was sort of exciting. Moving from school to school, I had to adapt very quickly. It made my social skills stronger and I had to be able to come out of my shell as a child. I didn't find school easy but I found ways of coping well and I found it easy to learn. I thought of school as active and fun.

I remember at primary school in Adelaide, we had two teachers, and they were both PE teachers. So, if we got our work done early we'd always go outside and play games. I clearly remember that was the reward, if we finished well and on time. That system worked for me growing up, and I still use it now. If I have a good training week, or a good patch of games, I'll do something I wouldn't usually do. You know, chocolate. Or lollies ...

I hate to think how I would have turned out if I'd not been good at sport, I really do. I'm very lucky. I know sport's not it for a lot of people, but you have to find the one thing that you're good at, or want to be good at, and work towards it. Anything like that motivates you to keep going. It's important to not go through things alone, to know that lots of others go through the same difficulties, and I really recommend talking to older people about finding things that work, to help you find your place at school.

Something I had growing up, and still have, is respect for elders. I think anybody who's had more time in the world has experience and life lessons to give. If you respect these people, and ask questions, you can get through, not unscathed, but with more information under your belt.

I definitely think it's a lot harder these days. There's so much out there that's distracting, and other forms of bullying that I just can't comprehend: Facebook, the internet, Twitter, texting. I think how horrible it would have been if someone had posted pictures of me on the internet – that the whole school could see – how that would have affected me. School can still be a good experience, but children need to engage with their family, friends and teachers to really succeed. They need that support.

I didn't realise at the time, but sport taught me a lot of life lessons. For one thing, you can never perfect anything, you can always improve. That drives me. I want to get the best out of myself, for me, my family and my team, and I'm disciplined and relentless about it. I learned to not take things for granted; opportunities don't come around too often, so you need to be in the right headspace to take them. The biggest thing sport's helped me with is leadership, and understanding what sport does not just for you, but for others. When you play professional sport, you have the opportunity to really inspire people, which is actually pretty cool.

Michael and myself set up our foundation as a vehicle to contribute back. We want to create more Indigenous role models, the next young Indigenous leader. We know how hard it was ourselves without support, in a disadvantaged community, to make it, so we are trying to make it a bit easier for other people. We have a target community down at the NSW – Victorian border and in Sydney, the ACT, WA and Adelaide. We've got six fully-paid university degrees at The University of Sydney, University of South Australia, Edith Cowan Univeristy, University of New South Wales and Western Sydney University and we are working with Year 8, 9, 10, and 11 kids to get them on scholarships to university. Because we all know that education is what's important – it's empowering and everything comes from there.

Growing up not knowing who I am has affected me a lot. It's a lifelong journey. I feel like I've missed out on a fantastic culture. I still believe I am part of it, but you know, not being able to speak the language, or know exactly what part of the Flinders Ranges we come from, or how big our extended family is, or where they are. I feel like I have been cheated a little bit from that point of view. But at the same time, I am very proud that we are still here, adapting, and we will always be here. The best thing about our culture is that we have been able to adapt and cope. But everybody is on a journey to figure out who they are and where they come from.

Ultimately the racial abuse didn't affect me so much because I didn't understand the drive behind what people were saying. I had my cousins on the outside of school calling me 'coconut'. I didn't even know what that meant. It wasn't until I started playing AFL, and being racially taunted there, that I really understood what was happening and stood up against it. That's when I said, 'That's wrong, you shouldn't say that. It actually hurts my feelings.' I went through a couple of mediation sessions with those players who vilified me to make sure they understood what they were talking about, and how it affects not just me, but my family and my extended family.

I've definitely learned to stand up for what I strongly believe in. I don't think that's negotiable.

STELLA
YOUNG

Born with osteogenesis imperfecta, a genetic condition that causes brittle bones, Stella Young zipped around in a wheelchair from the age of three. She described herself as having 'the structural integrity of an underbaked pavlova'. Mostly, though, Stella was a star.

She was the editor of the ABC's disability portal, a journalist, a broadcaster, a panelist on ABC TV1's *Q&A*, and a stand-up comic. Bold, bolshy, articulate, and charming, she was a warrior for disability rights who coined the phrase 'inspiration porn' and gave a Sydney TEDx Talk entitled 'I am not your inspiration, thank you very much'.

But at school in a small Victorian country town, Young expended her energy pretending she was 'normal', and dreaming of an able-bodied boyfriend and a berth in the cool girls' group.

She went on to self-identify as a 'crip', and was robustly unapologetic for not fitting other people's preconceptions of what disability should look like. She frocked up, made dirty jokes, danced, and lived her life to the fullest.

Stella credited her parents' no-nonsense approach to having a disabled child for her resilience and pragmatism. Being singled out and ostracised at school gave her the confidence to say 'screw fitting in'. Coupled with the skills she honed as a kid determined to blend in at all costs, she reacted with steely grace when idiots patted her on the head in public, or when Twitter trolls flamed her.

She was also damned funny. Stella died unexpectedly from an aneurysm in 2014, and the world is less bright because of it.

I wanted to be popular. Oh, I very much wanted to be one of those popular girls. I read *The Baby-Sitters Club*, and *Sweet Valley High*, all those books. They were about the girls who had strong friendships in clubs and groups, the popular crowd, and I wanted so much to be them. But I wasn't. Not even when I was hanging out with those girls, before they told me to go away.

At primary school I was the only kid with a disability of any kind, because I went to a very small country school. I was picked on a little bit by two girls in about Grade 3 or 4, but it was nothing major. They just decided they didn't want to be my friend, that's all, and would run away from me. But that kind of thing happens to all kids. I don't think it's right to say disability was necessarily the cause for me.

I can't say what difference it made being different, because I was never not different! I *think* my experience was pretty normal, well, apart from using a wheelchair and breaking bones. I've broken hundreds now. Hundreds and hundreds. I used to count the long bones, you know, not fingers and toes and stuff, but once I got to 350 or something, I was like, 'I'm going to stop counting. It's boring now.'

The breaks hurt as much for me as for anyone else, but I think I have a pretty high pain threshold. It's not the same as for other kids, though, because I was so used to it. I was calm. I still got really hot, felt a bit sick, in fact that's how I could tell if something was really broken or I'd just hurt myself a little. But even that got quite familiar.

I broke a bone a week, probably, when I was younger. I'd almost always have something broken. When I was seven I had to go home from a birthday party because a chip got stuck in my throat, I coughed, and my collarbone broke. But for me, that was pretty normal. Someone would yell out, 'Ring Stella's mum!' and everyone was, 'Righteo!' My parents would just bandage me up. It would've been ridiculous to take me to the hospital every time I broke something.

At high school, everything was about me just wanting to fit in with my non-disabled friends. I didn't want to be different. I didn't like hanging out with other people with disabilities. It wasn't until I was older, nearly at uni, that I went, 'There's value in this crip community thing.'

One of my biggest challenges was having to take the accessible route all the time. You know, you'd be walking to class together with friends, and invariably I'd have to duck off and find the accessible entrance, that kind of thing, and I'd get really worried about joining in the conversation again. I'd have missed huge chunks of the conversation, but I'd pretend I hadn't. I had no idea what was going on, but I'd be all, 'Oh, yes, yes. Of *course*.'

I spent a lot of time bluffing my way through things. I had to pretend to know what was going on at all times, because otherwise people would notice that I kept buggering off. And I didn't want people to think I was different.

My strategy, at all times, was to be no bother. I'd never ask anyone to go with me, because I was worried about being an imposition. I didn't want to put anyone out, or ask anybody to do anything to assist me, or express the need for any extra assistance, because then they might make the integration aide hang out with me, and *that*, as I'd learned in primary school, would be social suicide.

I'd hated the feeling of being watched, of having the bloody integration aide peering over me. I couldn't run off and be naughty like I thought the other kids were being. She was lovely, just doing her job, but I resented being different. Not so much the physical stuff – more that no one else was being watched, or looked after, or anything like that. I was being singled out. I hated that.

At high school there was an integration aide under my name, because I was the one who looked disabled enough for the school to get some funding, but I used to cringe when people referred to her as *my* aide. I was all, 'I don't need one of you, I don't need any help.' But there were kids with intellectual problems who didn't get funded because they didn't look 'funny' enough, so the aide was funnelled off to them. I think I saw her about three times. We had coffee, once, in Year 12.

It's different now, of course. An extra set of hands would be great! I wish I had an aide. To do my washing, unstack the dishwasher ...

I was always determined to keep up. To go to all the birthday parties and things. When I was a kid my parents made that happen, you know, portable ramps to get me into places. They encouraged me to do extracurricular things, like Brownies, which I did for about five minutes before I was completely bored. Yeah, you know, one of those kids, easily bored.

I didn't get many badges. They tried to give me pity badges, but I didn't want those. I wanted to *earn* them. But none of the things you could earn badges for, like, say, swimming, were accessible.

I don't think I had the hardest time in high school. I know other girls who were bullied mercilessly, much much worse than me, for absolutely no reason at all. But it happened. I'd gone to high school with my best primary school friend, Amy, and we stuck together through Years 7 and 8. But by the end of Year 8 we'd made friends with a whole bunch of girls, five or six of them, and they then decided they were going to kick me out of the group.

They literally sat me down one lunchtime, right at the end of the year, and said, 'We don't want you hanging out with us.' I was so distressed; I had the whole summer holidays to think about it, and stew and stress and be anxious about having no friends when I went back in Year 9.

It was down to this one girl, Frankie, who took a real dislike to me. She zeroed in on Amy, and, well, I don't know what her thought process was, but she got Amy to kick me out of the group. In hindsight I realise Amy was a very easily led girl. She'd kind of followed me around because I was the more dominant one in the friendship, so when there was another dominant personality with more people backing her up, Amy just kind of threw her hands up and went, 'Wooop!' and followed the path of least resistance.

Frankie was just a very mean girl. She'd walk away from me, or up the stairs, and look over her shoulder and give me a smirk, this smug, satisfied look. I just didn't want to be near her. She never physically threatened me, but she terrified me. I found her very frightening.

I don't know why she disliked me – my mum's theory was that it was because her parents were divorced and mine weren't. But then, that was my parents' great theory. Anytime me or my younger sisters got a hard time at school, my mum would say it was because people were jealous of the awesome parents we had. Which was, let's face it, very unlikely. Amusing, yes. But unlikely.

Looking back I wonder if absence solidified the loss of my place in that group. It might have. I had to do a lot on my own for disability reasons. I had surgery on my legs in Year 8, so I had to have time off school, and it was at the end of Year 8 they kicked me out. I also spent a lot of time with adults, and that's a common experience amongst people with disabilities; they mature quickly and get along with adults better than with their peers.

I remember I stressed all holidays, because I was terrified of having no friends. But of course I had to go back. My parents said, 'Just make new friends', which sounds so easy, but it's not easy when you're, y'know, fourteen years old, and you had a firm niche and then you lose it.

So I thought, 'Okay. Right, I'm going to try and sit with other people at lunchtimes.' And I floated around and sat with other people, and it felt really awkward. It's difficult to be subtle in a chair. I couldn't just slip in unnoticed. I was half expecting to be told to just go away, I was sure they were wondering what I was doing there.

Then I sort of thought, 'What the hell, I could be the worst house on the best street,' and I 'joined' the popular group. I'd go and sit with them, eat lunch, and hang out, until this mortifying incident one lunchtime. The girls were all talking about how they wished someone would go away. You know, 'I wish she'd just f**k off.' Of course, as usual, I didn't know who they were talking about. I was just agreeing like always, nodding and smiling, saying, 'I know, oh yes, I *know.*'

Eventually, yes, I realised they were talking about me. They wished *I* would just f**k off. So, I raised my chair up, and said, 'I'm just going to go to the toilet,' and I went. I wish I'd been more profound, but there it is. I did go to the toilet, and I cried. Obviously I couldn't go back, I couldn't sit with them again. So I had to float around *again* and try to find another group.

My high school year level was very cliquey, I think, and I'd been kicked out of two groups. It took a long time to stop caring about being popular; I kept pretending to be friends with the cool kids in the corridor.

I ended up hanging with some other girls. I wasn't close to them, but they didn't mind having me around, and I didn't *dislike* them. I think, when you come from a small school in a small town, you make friends by default because you're all thrown together. You're not necessarily like-minded, you just have to put up with each other until you can get out of there.

Amy did eventually apologise but not until a whole year later, at the end of Year 9. She began to be allowed to hang out with me one lunchtime a week, which, really, is hysterical. She'd said, 'I want to hang out with Stella, what do you think of that?' – and the group allowed her to have one 'Stella day' a week. At the time I was really grateful, but when I look at it now I think, '*What?!* How completely bizarre.'

I don't know if any of it had to do with disability, or being different. There was only one time they used disability as my weak spot and that was spreading rumours that I was incontinent and wore nappies. It seems ridiculous now, but at the time I was horrified by what people would think, and I thought, 'They've found it! The Achilles heel that will ruin my life!' but in the end nobody took that much notice.

A turning point was when I got my hair cut. My mum's a hairdresser, so you never got a cooling-off period if you had a bad hair day. Mum would just grab the scissors and say, 'I'll fix it.' *Most* people have to make an appointment and get to have a little think about what they want done, but not at our house. So I mentioned I was sick of my long hair, mum cut it short, and of course the next day at school I was a lesbian. Not just a girl with short hair, but, obviously, a lesbian.

So, there was a lot of whispering behind my back, then this girl asked loudly, 'So Stella, are you a lesbian now?', and I slammed my locker door and said, 'Why? Do you want to f**k me?' I'm sure it wasn't quite as awesome as it is in my head when I retell this story, but I do remember being proud of my comeback, of finally standing up for myself. I think it made me finally realise I didn't give a f**k anymore. I was nearly out of there. I was doing well.

I was anxious for school to be over. I was anxious not to be a kid anymore. I was *hanging* to get out of there. I didn't give a shit about being popular by the end. I knew that once I moved away from Stawell, and got to uni, that I was going to have friends who I'd chosen. Not people I was stuffed together with in a small town. I knew there was a big world out there.

I was more relaxed in Year 12. I was a little bit friends with lots of people and Amy was allowed to have more than one 'Stella day' a week. She'd eventually realised it was an odd regime to be obeying. Also, by then, I could see the light at the end of the tunnel. School, after all, was something I just had to get through.

I had a plan and an exit strategy. I did two Year 12 subjects in Year

11, so then I had less to do in Year 12. Having a plan was important; because the whole thing about being a kid with a disability in a small town is that you don't know what's possible, because no one's like you. You've got no role models.

I'd made a good friend when I was fifteen, Caroline, a woman ten years older who had the same genetic condition as me. I asked my parents if I could stay with her in Melbourne and I'd catch the V/Line train down and spend weekends in her apartment. She had such a wonderful group of friends from all over the place and I met lots of them. From uni, from work, from the crip community – so I met heaps of people with disability and was introduced to the whole crip scene. That ended up being really important; I learned there's a wonderful bond that comes from shared experience.

Just seeing Caroline do her thing – living and working and getting around on her own – helped me relax a lot, because it gave me a bigger picture. I realised school was temporary, and living independently was doable. 'Oh, okay, worst case scenario I'll do exactly what she does.' So I was doing things to put that in place.

I did what I needed to do. I remember being confident that if I did subjects I liked it would lead to a career that I liked. So when the teachers tried to talk me into doing specialist maths to get higher scores – and I *hated* maths – I was like, 'Nah, I'm not up for that.' I wanted to do biology and psych. I didn't *need* a very high score to get into what I wanted, which was Arts/Journalism at Deakin, so I didn't worry about it. And I did quite well. I was dux of my school.

The resilience I've learned, I got, I think, from my parents. I was their first child, and they didn't have any expectations of what any kid of theirs was going to be like, or do, so they just got on with it and took it all in their stride. They got a bit sad when the doctors said I would probably die but apart from that they were like, 'This is fine. This is totally alright.'

They were told not to have more children, but by the time they found out there wasn't a risk, that my condition was caused by a point mutation, they'd had two more. They just decided I wasn't that bad after all, that two more of me was a risk they were willing to take.

They certainly didn't expect less of me. When I was in high school, a lovely lady from the local community wanted to nominate me for some kind of achievement award. My parents wouldn't have it. They went, 'Well, she hasn't really achieved much though, has she?' and the woman said, 'No, no, she's an inspiration!' But all I was doing was getting good marks, there was nothing exceptional about it. She just reckoned it was a bloody good effort because I was doing it sitting down.

People with disability are called 'inspirational' all the time, and it doesn't feel like the compliment it's supposed to be. If someone calls me an inspiration for going to work on the train, it's like, okay, you find me inspirational because I'm more than you expect. Which is nothing. So when I'm just a normal person, suddenly I'm an 'inspiration'. That doesn't actually feel good, it feels condescending and othering.

Part of the reason for my dropping Brownies, I think, was my mother's lack of enthusiasm for Brown Owl. Brownies was held in the local Scout hall, and the Scout hall didn't have a ramp, so when I started going to Brownies they got the Lions club to donate money and build one. Brown Owl wanted me to be in a photo in the paper with the ramp. And my parents said, 'No, it's for the whole community, not for Stella, and you are not using her as a poster child for charity.' From then on there was a bit of tension between mum and Brown Owl ...

I also think that once I got the confidence that it was going to be alright, I hung on to that. It's given me confidence as an adult. It's made me confident enough to not necessarily care if people don't like me. I'm strong enough to say what I want to say and not be bothered if people don't like it. My experiences, I think, have made me much more resilient in standing up for what I think is the right thing.

Because, actually, there are lots of people who don't like me. Lots of people in the disability community, for example, because I make it my business to challenge stereotypes of people with disabilities. I question stuff like that 'inspirational' trope, that many disabled people are, frankly, quite comfortable with, and live off. There's a whole industry of inspirational speakers who trade on overcoming adversity, and when I say, 'It's bullshit', people don't like it very much.

I have absolutely learned that pretending you know what's going on doesn't work. It changes your life when you admit that you don't know. It gives you the gift of fully understanding things rather than just glossing over. I think a lot of adults still do that, pretend they know everything.

Frankie still works in a shop in Stawell. It's completely irrational but when I go home I can't quite bring myself to walk down the street and not feel the threat. Which is ludicrous. I'm a 31-year-old woman, and I'm very successful in my career and in my life. I have great friends and people who love me, and there is nothing she can take from me now, nothing, and yet I still have anxiety that I might run into her.

It strikes me, as an adult, that the experiences we look back on are so subjective. When I was on *Q&A* the first time, one of the girls from the popular group – one of the ones who told me to 'f**k off' that lunchtime – wrote a message on my Facebook wall, and private messaged me, to say, 'It was so great to see you on *Q&A* tonight. I'm incredibly proud of you and I'm so sad I didn't get to know you better in high school.'

And I was like, 'What! Are you f**king kidding me? You knew me. You *hated* me.' When she said 'I wish I'd gotten to know you better', I thought, 'I bet you frigging do!' I replied, 'Well, thank you, that's very generous of you,' and that's all. But I talked about it in an interview that ended up on the internet, and she saw *that* and got in touch again and said, 'I just saw this interview and I had no idea that you felt that way. I don't know what to say except that I'm really sorry, and people grow up.'

I thought it was so interesting that I wasn't even a blip on her radar. I was just someone that she didn't get to know very well, and to me, it was devastating. And I find that confusing because she was very dominant in that girls' group. So maybe she was mean to me because she was mean to a lot of people, but I wasn't particularly important, you know? It's fascinating how subjective it all is. Maybe *I* gave that experience to other people? Maybe *I* was dismissive and mean. I just don't know. I do know that at school, back then, it's all about you. Now I have more empathy to think what other people might be experiencing.

Another thing my parents said all along was, 'This seems like a big deal now, but it won't be a big deal when you're an adult.' I never believed them, of course, but they were completely right.

Interestingly, I never felt physically vulnerable, or that I had to protect myself. This is partly because when you're younger, your self-image is totally different from what you actually look like. I was surrounded by people who looked normal, so my self-image was created off them, not from not being able to go up the steps after them. I think it takes hanging out with lots of people with different body types to accept who you actually are.

Also, I have what I call 'wheelchair privilege', and by that I mean I'm not ridiculed because of my disability in the way that other short statured people are. A wheelchair signifies 'serious' disability, so we're taken more seriously. But a while ago, a short statured person was set on fire at a footy function, and a friend of mine was in the city the week after that and someone screamed at him, 'Yeah! Set him on fire!' If you're my size in the world, and walking, then you're fair game.

I've got a really high tolerance for offence now. I can't remember what it would feel like to be offended. A woman on the train a while back came up and asked me if I had a vagina. That was bemusing. I also have a lot of interaction with children because they find me fascinating. A boy once asked me if I was 'imaginary', and I thought that was beautiful.

Now I celebrate being a bit 'other'. People ask all the time, 'But wouldn't you prefer not to have a disability? Be an able-bod?' And the answer's 'Nope. No way.' I really like who I am, and what disability has taught me. A lot of the strengths in my life come from disability, and very few of the weaknesses do.

There are so many things I like about being me that hinge on me having a disability. I'm resilient. I'm a really natural problem solver. I'm confident. If I didn't have a disability I wouldn't be who I am. I'd be someone else, who I'm sure would be nice, but I wouldn't be *me*.

MO'JU

Mojo Ruiz de Luzuriaga, the Wiradjuri Filipino musician and performer known professionally as Mo'Ju, understands the complexities of identity and not fitting in better than most. Queer, non-binary, Dubbo-born with observant Catholic parents and of Filipino, European and Wiradjuri heritage, Mo'Ju has had plenty of opportunity to ponder the many ways they do not and did not belong, particularly when they were parachuted into one small, racist primary school after another – the perpetual 'non-white, resolutely non-girly new girl'.

Mo'Ju's true home is music, a legacy from their worldly, musical grandparents. It was their escape and a haven of constancy and joy. They took lessons, learned clarinet and guitar, sang in the church choir and holed up in their bedroom writing songs. Mo'Ju's trajectory as a fierce and unwavering artist and songwriter is intimately entwined with an interrogation of identity, family history and race politics. 'Native Tongue', Mo'Ju's multi-award-winning song from the album of the same name, is a profound grieving for loss of culture. It gave Australia and the music industry whiplash, and cut to the heart of our country's uneasy relationship with race and acceptance.

Early on, Mo'Ju was told they didn't fit the pop-star mould. Their response was to stop trying to fit. Their EP *O.K.* is about mental health; the song 'Ghost Town', a collaboration with Joelistics, explores personal ghosts. Mo'Ju has become a unique, intelligent and fascinating artist – a direct result of their lifelong ache for belonging, and the experiences with school and family that gave them their determination to be, unapologetically, themself.

I was born in Dubbo, or 'the big smoke', in Central West NSW. Mum is half Wiradjuri, so that's her home, and my grandparents lived there, so we gravitated towards Dubbo as a base. Dad was an ambulance officer and regularly transferred, and I'd be dropped off with my grandparents each time while my parents set up a new house in a new town and enrolled us in yet another new Catholic primary school.

On Mum's side of the family were a lot of musicians, and my relationship with my grandparents Pidgie and Albert was special. They gave me a jazz education. Pop played cornet and was so proud of his record collection – Billie Holiday and Louis Armstrong were like saints in that house – and there was an organ there that I'd sit at and hit the keys on. My guitar was my aunty's hand-me-down. My grandmother was a soprano, Mum played trombone. It's where my music came from.

And I could talk to them. One time some kids were doing slanty eyes at me, 'ching chong Chinaman' stuff, and I went to my grandmother. I was so upset. I wasn't even Chinese! And she totally flipped my perspective.

She said, 'There's nothing wrong with being Chinese. Chinese people are beautiful,' and pulled out the *World Book Encyclopedia* – no internet then – and read to me about Chinese culture and showed me pictures. I was like, 'Oh. That's rad.' When kids called me Chinese after that, I was cool. Like, 'Whatever'. Sometimes they called me Japanese, and I'd tell them I loved Japan because they had a cool culture. I'd say, 'Have you seen *The Karate Kid*? Karate is from Japan. I'm so into it.' My parents and I didn't talk like that. We didn't share. You just learned to be tough. My therapist asked how I was taught to talk about my emotions, and I just laughed. We didn't.

My primary years really were all over the place: Lithgow, Bathurst, Wellington, Dunedoo, Baradine and then back to Dubbo. I never settled and was always the new kid in town. Dad is Filipino and our surname is big, long and Spanish: Ruiz de Luzuriaga. No one could say it and no one wanted to try.

I didn't mind moving, in that we were always leaving somewhere I hated. The hardest for me was Baradine. We were there two years, from when I was eight, and I spent most of it pleading to leave. It's tiny, population 500, and that included anyone living within twenty kilometres of town. The school was 30 or 40 kids: kindergarten, Year 1 and Year 2 together in one classroom, Years 3 and 4 next door, Years 5 and 6 in the room beside that.

As far as I remember, I was the only kid who wasn't white, and I was harassed every day. They'd flip their chairs as I walked past so I'd trip over, and kids would follow me home and throw rocks at me. Every. Single. Day. Every racial slur an eight-year-old can think of. It was a minefield of shit to navigate. I was *that* kid. And my parents would say, 'Why don't you make friends?'

The rejection was very direct. When my parents went to someone's house, I'd go with, and there'd be kids from school who I desperately wanted to like me, and we'd play. And come Monday, they'd totally blank me: 'Who are you?' Dad's friends called him 'A to Z' because they couldn't pronounce his actual name and would joke about him being a 'boat person'. The way to be kind of accepted was clearly to make yourself the butt of the joke. It's the 'model migrant' mentality. Make fun of yourself and you're rewarded with, 'You're one of the good ones.' On the surface, cool, because who doesn't want to be the funny guy and be liked? But it's a lot of racism to internalise.

Certain teachers also singled me out. One time the kids glued my books to my desk and thumbtacks to my seat. So I was in trouble for not sitting down. Then the teacher said, 'Okay, move over here', so I picked up the books and the cover tore off one of them because it was glued to the table, and she just dragged me out of class and caned me across my palms and the back of my legs. I said it wasn't me and she said, 'Don't be a tattletale.' Was that just some straight-up racism? I don't know for sure. But, yeah. Probably.

Once in music class the teacher took us outside to learn a piece on guitar, said we should each find a place to sit and practise. While I was playing, the principal came up and demanded to know why I was there. I said I'd been told to. The principal called me a liar. I got the cane.

It was brutal. At some point you realise you're not heard. And if you're punished either way, what's the point in compliance? Perhaps it's why I'm so stubborn, determined to do things my own way.

Belonging, and wanting to belong, is such a complicated idea. It's why those of us who've had trauma through school often find outsider communities and go into the arts. It's the promise of a place where you can be accepted. We didn't have Triple J then, but we had *Video Hits* and *Rage*. And, wow ... There they were, in music videos: people of colour, queer people, on my television.

I'd escape to play music in my bedroom. I loved it. Music was *mine.* I entertained myself for hours playing guitar, writing songs, teaching myself multi-tracking using a dual tape deck. I enjoyed figuring things out. I'd record a song off the radio, listen to it over and over and work it out by ear. Then you impress someone by playing a song from the radio! Kids seek out approval, and it was that simple at first. It wasn't deep, until it was, and songwriting became processing, somewhere to put feelings I couldn't express or share. There were some emo, angsty songs early in my teens. I'm sort of thankful I lost the cassettes along the way ...

Home was kind of lonely. Mum was commuting from Baradine to Dubbo for work, coming back for the weekends. Dad was always on call. My older brother, who I adored, is eleven years older than me and had already moved out, and my other brother, five years younger, was still little. I remember once waking in the middle of night, sneaking into the lounge room to watch TV, and the film *Purple Rain* was on. It was so 'not suitable', but I was magnetised. Prince was a revelation. The answer to questions I didn't even know I was asking. I sat there going, 'What *is* this? Oh my *god.*' I didn't understand anything, but I *loved* it. I wanted to *be* that: a person wearing platform shoes and heaps of make-up, who I was pretty sure was a man? Of *course* that's what I was going to do.

I escaped into Prince-inspired fantasies. 'I'm going to be so f**king fabulous that everyone will be like, "Shit, I'm stuck in the middle of nowhere, and that person we tormented is on TV."' It sounds maniacal now, but it drove me, that sweet revenge fantasy.

I'd always been theatrical, playing dress-ups. I didn't have language for it, but knew I was queer from a really young age. For a while in kindergarten, I decided my name was Nicholas and made everyone call me that. I thought I'd marry the girl next door. For a school assignment I wrote, 'On Mother's Day, I surprised Mum by dressing up like a girl instead of a boy to go to mass. When we got back, I changed into the clothes of boys. Then we had a Mother's Day party.' And I'd drawn myself in a dress. My gift for Mum was to dress up like a girl.

I was uncompromising on who I was. I liked martial arts and basketball and *Ghostbusters*. I had a Mr T action figure. I wasn't interested in little-girl things; I wanted to play with the boys, and I wasn't conforming to the gender binary. My parents gave me the classic 'China-doll' Asian-kid haircut – a bob with bangs and jet-black hair – and I wanted it shorter, but they played me. I was into *Masters of the Universe*, and they told me it was a He-Man haircut. I was like, '*Yeah*, it's a battle fringe.'

In Year 3 or 4, kids told me I was a lesbian. I didn't know what it meant, but it sounded bad. As a teen, I was like, 'Okay, I know what that means now, and it's probably true, but I don't feel safe to admit it.' It's tough knowing you're queer and being on a parallel journey of Catholicism. I had genuine concerns about hell. It sounds silly to me now, but it was a real question for me. I heard Nick Cave's *Murder Ballads* when I was fourteen or fifteen, when I was seriously questioning my faith. And I thought, 'Damn, this is good. But, man, it's *evil*.' I was scared that liking it meant going to hell.

One time I was in the car with a band friend I was out to. Mum was driving, maybe taking us to church, and she was saying some very homophobic things that were obviously informed by her religion and that she would be mortified by now, and my friend was looking at me like, 'Oh man, I'm so sorry.'

Mum's been married to a woman for over a decade now. When she came out, I was excited and happy for her, but part of me was pretty pissed. I'd been through hell! When I was sixteen, seventeen and came out to my parents, they took me to the priest. As in, 'We're not having this conversation; you can talk to the priest.' Fortunately the priest was cool and suggested a counsellor, and the counsellor was like, 'You're actually fine. You're just gay.' But it's hard to shake Catholic guilt; I've never entirely been able to move past it.

But I knew who I was at my core, and wasn't going to compromise. The mum of one of my school friends pulled me aside once, saying she'd heard I was a lesbian, and it was a shame I was going to hell, but they had groups that could help if I wanted. And I remember replying that I was all good thanks: 'I don't want to be saved.'

I had to fight hard to go to the public high school in Dubbo. My primary schools were all Catholic, and I wanted a new start away from my bullies. I was adamant. Dad was never thrilled and kept threatening to pull me out and send me to a Christian boarding school. He'd say things like, 'You're going to end up pregnant.' And I'm like, 'I promise you, I'm not.'

My mental health as a teenager wasn't great. I had a lot of shame and fear, depression and anxiety. I was hiding my queerness from home and school, and keeping secrets about yourself isolates you. And there weren't many people in Dubbo that looked like me; no one else had my cultural background. A lot of the time it felt like I didn't fit anywhere.

There's a big Indigenous community there, but my history's complicated and I didn't grow up with much access to it. Some people saw me as Blak, but to others I wasn't Blak enough. A lot presumed I was Chinese because they thought of all Asians as one and the same.

Some people even thought I was First Nations American. A lot of people didn't know what I was, but they knew I was brown. There are a few Filipinos in Dubbo and my brother's best friend was Pinoy, but I didn't have that. People like me weren't on TV. I didn't look like the people that other people had crushes on. So it's like, 'Well, I'm not that then.' You feel ugly and ashamed, and you keep parts of yourself hidden.

I was fourteen when I first confided in a school friend that I was queer. The next day when I rocked up to school, I was outed and everybody knew. That was scary. It was a big high school, about eight hundred kids, and it made me feel extremely unsafe. I was the only openly queer person and I was terrorised a bit after that. Not just name-calling. Boys spat on me. Probably some girls, too. People I didn't necessarily know from school were like, 'I know about you. I know who you are.' People were mean, things turned mean, sometimes it got violent.

There's not much to do in Dubbo, so we all were in bands and put on big weekend events. At one concert I spotted a girl I knew from a different high school and went up to say hello. I put my hand on her shoulder and said, 'Hey, how you doing?' She turned and said, 'Don't touch me, you f**king dyke.' It was a whole scene. People were standing around watching; one of them called me a 'f**king faggot'. Then the girl punched me in the face, and I punched her back. Two tough goth girls from my school came over and asked if I was okay, and it felt good that they had my back. I started to walk away and then the girl pulled my hair and punched me in the back of the head. For the first time I realised, 'Wow, there are people who actually feel threatened by me.'

It changed by the time I graduated. More people I knew were

coming out or experimenting with their sexuality and I became a bit more popular. I'd been the 'only gay in the village' for a very long time, and then by the time we were seniors, most people had gotten over their shit and there weren't so many factions anymore. It was like we'd been into battle together making it through high school and by the end we were all on the same side and most of us were friends – or at the very least friendly – no matter how unlikely.

I had a place, a group of friends, and for that I'm grateful. There were the geeks, the freaks and the jocks, and I was definitely in the 'freaks'. We were an odd bunch, the misfits, every race and religion, and we were reputed to be the 'drugs, sex and rock-and-roll' crew. We weren't really as rebellious as people thought, but the true part was we mostly all played in bands.

I was goofy and funny, so despite all the bullying and stuff, not all the jocks hated me. People mostly liked me. The geeks had it worse, because the freaks were considered weird but sort of edgy, so we weren't getting tormented in the way they were, just for playing *Dungeons & Dragons* or for being teacher's pets and getting straight As.

Everyone was being tormented by one another, I now realise. Everyone's bullied at some point. If you don't have trauma from high school, I think you probably peaked too soon.

In hindsight, I'm grateful to have had those experiences, because they made me who I am. It's made me the artist I am. It's a huge part of the music I make and the stories I have to tell. It's made me uncompromising, and you have to be to stay true. I learned resilience and to accept myself. All of it informs who you are.

I've found being an outsider gives you perspective. You learn to observe other people; you learn to trust your instincts and be discerning. It's made me compassionate. Everyone has full internal lives and you don't know what's going on for someone else.

I'm still working out who I am, where I fit and what's been lost. It's super complex. I have some white heritage, but I've never been perceived as white, or felt accepted by that community, so I don't identify there. I have a complicated relationship with my Wiradjuri heritage. I'm proud of it, I have deep respect for my Elders and my ancestors, but I also tread lightly. I've been granted more access to my cultural heritage as a Filipino in a way I probably can never have access to Wiradjuri spaces, so I lean into it more. It's a stronger bond.

I dedicated *Native Tongue* to my grandmother Pidgie. So much of that album is about her story, and my grandparents' love story. Pidgie is Wiradjuri and sang soprano, and she wanted to sing at the Opera House one day. She didn't get to because she had to stay in Dubbo and look after her mum. When I finally performed at the Opera House, and sang 'Native Tongue' it was such a big deal, such a big moment.

Music is absolute freedom. It's like, all things at once. It can be confessional and introspective and personal and emotional, or it can be purely entertainment and fun and experimental. And it can be cultural and communal and unifying. When I was a teenager, playing in bands was a way of bonding with other kids. Music brings people together. And it can be completely solo and for no one else but yourself. For me, it's always been just joy.

I'm so lucky that music is part of my family, that we share it. My younger brother, Stevie, plays drums with me. We're really close. Neither of us fitted in as kids, but we had each other. He's my most consistent collaborator over the years. We write songs together, have toured together – it's cool to have experiences together on the road.

Even though Prince was a major influence on me, I no longer want to *be* Prince. Not that I *could* have been – he was a prodigy, one-in-a-million talent. But it's also true that I no longer have that 'F**k you all, I'm going to be a star' aspiration. Fame is not the life for me. I'm in music to write songs and make art and do work that's fulfilling and challenging and creative. The modest public exposure I've had showed me, 'Oh, this isn't fun.' Your privacy is compromised, and there's much to be said for anonymity when you're walking down the street. I don't need to be exposed to random people's opinions about my facial hair.

But I do know it's important that I'm visible. Because, well, apart from Prince, there weren't many people for me to look at as a kid and say, 'Oh! That's me!' So the more wholly myself I am, the more it might help someone who feels isolated to feel a little more seen. Or to feel they can be whatever they want. The idea that there's value to what I'm doing, that I'm helping, gives me a real sense of purpose. It's important to me to give back. It feels self-important to say that, but it's not. It was really lonely. If I can help anyone else feel less like that, then that's awesome.

That's much more interesting to me than getting likes on social media, being popular. Social media is like high school in many ways, and, having been bullied, I can see what's going on. I've got boundaries now. It's like, 'Why am I fighting with someone I don't know on screen? This is ridiculous.'

I believe in engaging in political conversation and I have a responsibility to use my platform to get word out on important issues. But when that starts having a negative impact on my private life and my mental health, I step away. I back off social media, delete it from my phone, and it's really liberating.

A huge part of what I do is kicking down doors. There's been a cultural shift in the last ten years, and hopefully the experiences I had as a younger person won't have to be relived by someone else. I almost left music. The feedback I used to get was that I wasn't the right kind of brown or queer to sell records. I wasn't attractive enough. I didn't look right or sound right. But I've made a career based on not conforming and writing about what's important to me, and I'm really proud of that.

The industry wants to pigeonhole and say, 'You're *this* type of artist,' which is all about how to market you. And I'm like, 'F**k off.' I am whatever type of artist I wake up feeling like. The whole point is to evolve and create something new. Yes, I'm definitely into soul and jazz, and I like to pay homage to what's gone before, but I'm not about 'doing a genre'. I'm interested in writing songs and whatever serves the song. There are all these intersecting parts of my identity, and music's no different. Music is an expression of the self.

I'm not trying to fit in. I never fitted in, so I'm not trying to do that now. I'm determined to follow my own path, and not having fitted in keeps me trying. I'm ambitious. I want people to hear my music and say, 'I know exactly who that is.' I don't want to be compared to someone else; if anything, I want to be an artist who people compare things *to*. Maybe I won't get there, but it's the journey I'm on. I'm good with that, I'm resolved in that.

Even in my twenties, I just wanted people to like me. I don't worry about that anymore. I don't like everyone I meet and that's okay. I can be argumentative and opinionated, and that's fine too. People don't have to agree. What I care about is respect. To earn people's respect is much better than being liked. It's taken a while, but it's a really nice place to get to.

JUDITH
LUCY

It's no secret that the ruthlessly self-deprecating comedian Judith Lucy had a challenging upbringing. Her first bestseller, *The Lucy Family Alphabet*, is a literal A to Z of a bizarre childhood more properly found in a bookshop's fantasy section. Few families, for instance, keep their cat in a cage on the dinner table. As an ex-Catholic and comic, Judith's metier has always been the confessional, and the connection between her career, and a childhood requiring mad skills to navigate, is easily drawn.

School was a vital respite from troubles at home, and as such Judith needed it too much. She used humour to defuse tense family situations, so moseyed along okay in the classroom, but while most kids experience bullying as rejection from the pack, Judith's emotional neediness locked her into a toxic close friendship that shredded her.

Drawn to sensitive topics, Judith's award-winning shows have traversed intense personal territory: getting fired from Austereo, hiring a gigolo, the death of her brother, betrayal, drinking, and the Christmas when her sister-in-law blurted out that Judith was adopted. Her second book, *Drink, Smoke, Pass Out*, is a droll search for meaning. Her ongoing show with Denise Scott is called *Disappointments*, her ABC podcast is *Overwhelmed and Dying*, and her 2020 stand-up show was *Judith Lucy Vs Men*. You will notice a theme.

One of Australia's most loved and divisive talents, Judith's gift is to hold trauma in her hand, and transmute it with humour. Her latest memoir, released in 2021, is *Turns Out, I'm Fine*.

I was a bit of a sensitive kid. Absolutely. If someone didn't like me I took it incredibly personally. I immediately went, 'What's wrong with me?' And I think bullies pick up on that. It took a long time to work out that everyone's got their own shit and everyone's just trying to do their best.

From a pretty early age when I'd hear that phrase, 'Your schooldays are the best days of your life,' I'd think, 'Well, I'd better blow my brains out then.' Even though I was a fan of school, I'd just think, 'It's got to get better than this, doesn't it?' But I loved school itself because when I was there, I wasn't at home.

Mum and dad argued every night, so I invested a lot in school and my school friendships. But I was shy, and ill-equipped to deal with people. I never went to kindergarten because Mum was under-confident socially, and kept me at home. She didn't think it was important for me to socialise with kids, didn't realise it was a big deal for me when I started school. I'd only ever mixed with adults, and when I was thrown into this environment of 26 girls and four boys, I had no idea how to relate to them. I found it very difficult.

A girl who was a year older than me sussed this out pretty quickly, and in the first month or so she just scared the hell out of me. She came up to me in the playground and basically said, 'You have to stand here, in this circle, and if you move I'll hurt you.' I was six, absolutely terrified, and I'd spend every recess and lunchtime standing in this circle and not moving. I finally broke down and told my mother, and she went down to the school and talked to someone and it stopped, but the fear didn't really go away.

I must admit I was struck by the 'sink or swim-ness' of school pretty quickly. I had a strong survival instinct, I think, and worked out early that you just had to get along with people. I put a lot of effort in. It made *Desperate Housewives* look like a walk in the park: god, the intrigue. Mary-Anne was my best friend for a while, and she left me for Karen, and then I became friends with Natalie, and before I knew it she'd run off with Narelle.

You just had to have a group to hang out with and I think I was also pretty desperate for a 'best' friend. Mum and Dad were wrapped up in their own world so, hey, I guess I started looking for love in all the wrong places. It wasn't until Grade 2 that I made a proper friend, Amber*, and in hindsight she was, er, a bit of a monster. We used to play these imaginary games where she was the witch, and myself and this other girl played her underlings, and she was just vile to us. She was a cow, actually, and my best friend for years, until the third year of high school.

After we got past primary she wasn't obviously horrible anymore, she just didn't do a lot for my self-esteem. She was my antithesis. She was cool, she got breasts before everyone else, she wore make-up, went out with boys and got drunk. I was just a really uptight over-achiever.

---

* not her real name.

A goody-good. The reality was there was so much conflict at home that I saw no point in adding to it. Why on earth would I want to inspire more shouting? I kept my head down, really, until after uni when I moved to Melbourne, and then it was 'Woohoo!'

I always wound up being a good friend to Amber's boyfriends. I was Janeane Garofalo in *The Truth about Cats & Dogs*. I was always the funny best friend who wasn't the one the boys wanted to go out with. They'd turn to me and say, 'You know, if I wasn't with Amber ...'

When I was thirteen or fourteen, she said one of those lines that stays with you forever: 'You know Judith, you're *really* not attractive. But you have got a good personality.'

To the day he died my father asked after her. 'How's *Amber*?' he'd say. I'd tell him, 'I haven't seen her in years, and you know what? She didn't treat me that well.' but it was always the same, 'How's that *Amber*? I *loved* that Amber.'

It was weird, because in many ways I did well. I had the lead in the school play, I was much better academically than her and yet ... I don't know. She had something over me for a long time. It wasn't until late high school that I made another friend, who I genuinely got on with, and suddenly my eyes were opened. I finally realised what a true friendship could be like. I have to admit though, it does take two to tango; I mean I let myself be treated like that and she must have had her own crap going on to have behaved in that way.

You know what? In hindsight, I think with all close relationships, be it a friend or partner, they obviously bring something out in you – for good or for bad – that you want on some level. I guess I just didn't feel very good about myself, and she really confirmed that for me.

The 'Amber pattern' kept repeating for a while, to be honest. I used to gravitate to these intense friendships which were very toxic, where I'd constantly be seeking approval from someone who wasn't ever going to give it to me. They'd be dealing it out, and I'd keep coming back for more. Fortunately I wised up a few years back.

It's interesting. One of the worst decisions I made in my entire life – and I've made a few – was to go to my school reunion. It didn't help that I'd just been sacked by Austereo and my confidence was at rock bottom. I thought, 'It'll be fun, and it's been twenty years,' and yet within five minutes of walking into the room I was like, 'Oh no! The reason I didn't keep in touch with any of you people is you're *all* a pack of bitches.' Okay, that's obviously an exaggeration. It was nice to see some of them but there was a lot of gossiping going on.

A lot of them were treating me oddly, kind of ignoring me, and eventually one woman walked up and said, 'Have you noticed that some of us aren't talking to you?' I said, 'Yes', and she said, 'You remember, six years ago, a bunch of us came to see your show, and we sent you a note and you didn't come out and have a drink with us?'

And you know what? I did remember that, and I explained that I hadn't come out with them because that was the night after my father disowned me, and he died six weeks later and he never spoke to me again. And she broke down and started hugging me like a crazy person, saying, 'Oh I knew there'd be a reason',' and I was thinking, 'This is insane.'

I saw Amber and went up and said, 'You do realise this is what happened?' And she made me, I swear to god, juggle. Just stood there with this look on her face, and at one point casually said, 'Yeah, I heard about your parents dying, *sorry* about that.' It was like I'd gone back in time. I was trying to please her, trying to justify myself, trying to *explain*. Finally a friend grabbed me, and we left. I was sobbing, crying, and all this stuff welled up in me. Years of being treated badly, and I let myself go back there again. I couldn't believe it.

It's really, really annoying, but one thing that happens in life is that when bad shit happens to you, you always get something out of it. It's incredibly irritating that as you get older you realise that every cliché is true. You know how you're supposedly meant to learn from failing? Aggravatingly, it's spot on.

And, it's another cliché, but having a sense of humour is what got me through. Being able to crack jokes and make people laugh made life easier all round. Humour was a huge part of my relationship with Amber. Nothing made me feel better than making her laugh, and I used to make her laugh all the time. I was clearly chasing her approval. I created things I knew she thought were funny. There were these superhero characters, called Captain Weakling and Bog, and sometimes I'd turn up at her place dressed as Captain Weakling. I'd perform songs to try and make her laugh. I'd get a huge buzz out of doing it for her.

I'm not sure where a sense of humour comes from. Dad had a fantastic sense of humour, yet I reckon he was a bit of a bully. My mother was a lot smarter than Dad, I realised, but had no sense of humour whatsoever. But Dad just seemed to be having a lot more fun than her. He found life genuinely amusing. Maybe I did go, 'That's a great coping mechanism.'

I can see comedy as an extension of the survival instinct. For a long time I did comedy because I wanted approval. Obviously I was craving something, wanting the love from my parents that they weren't very good at showing. I eventually worked out that comedy will never fill that hole.

I look back on it all and feel very differently about it now. I loved my parents and they loved me. But it wasn't an easy childhood. Mum put me on all these crazy diets from when I was eight, so when I went to other people's houses I'd eat like a maniac. We'd watch some television, and then, as opposed to everyone else in my year, I wasn't allowed to stay the night. She was weirdly over-protective. Two hours after dinner and mum would be at the door.

There was no point trying to hide my home situation. I went to the same school for twelve years – people already knew how 'interesting' my parents were. But I saw uni as a new beginning, and when someone would drop me home, I'd always say, 'Oh, anywhere around here,' blocks from where I lived.

I remember a friend being left alone in the kitchen, reaching into the cupboard to pull out a coffee cup and literally screaming. Because mum had put a cup back on the shelf several weeks ago with coffee still in it, and it was this fetid ... That would happen all the time. Mum wasn't big on housekeeping. I just wanted to get people out of the house as soon as possible.

I think, also, in terms of my career, because I came from an extraordinarily secretive family, my reaction has been to go tell everything. There were so many things that were never spoken about, like me being adopted. Maybe a part of my brain's missing, but when I hear that someone's a very private person, I always think, 'Why? What's the point? We're all in this shit together. We all f**k up. We all make mistakes. We've all got skeletons in the closet. Let's talk about it.'

This industry has been very kind to me. And if I hadn't had

the difficulties, and the massive insecurity and desperate need for approbation, I maybe wouldn't have gone into it, and I wouldn't have been so driven. I've worked some stuff out now, there's a level of desperation I used to have that I don't have anymore, and I can enjoy the good stuff about being a comedian. Maybe the way I got here wasn't so great, but where I am now is really good. I genuinely do love making people laugh.

My brother, Niall, is older than me and when I came to the end of school I told him how sad I was, convinced I'd miss everyone. And he said, 'No you won't. You'll never see most of those people again. Your friends will be the ones you meet at uni, because you'll share the same interests.' And I was going, 'No! No! Nooo! I'll be friends with all these people forever!'

And, of course, he was entirely correct.

BENJAMIN
LAW

The most important requirements for writerly success, apart from knowing where to shove an apostrophe, is having a mission and something to write about. Benjamin Law, a Sydney-based writer, humourist and broadcaster who's been called Australia's David Sedaris, is fuelled by decades lived on the outer.

Ben grew up a runty kid in a large, broken family, dealing with being Asian on the then whiter-than-white Gold Coast. He survived school by exhaustively camouflaging his homosexuality behind a complex smokescreen of walking straight, talking straight, acting straight, and loudly insisting that he wanted to shag Buffy the Vampire Slayer.

His first book, *The Family Law*, adapted into an SBS TV series, contains affectionate and hilarious essays about his extravagantly eccentric family. His second, *Gaysia*, took him through gay, lesbian and transgender communities in South-East Asia, and explores what it means to be gay in less queer tolerant countries.

Ben's intent is to trailblaze for the next generation of misfits. At school he was gasping for something that normalised difference, and he's pleased to write for anyone challenged by the hot mess of sexual identity, race and schoolyard politics. In 2019 he was named one of the Asian-Australian Leadership Summit's most Influential Asian-Australians, and one of *Harper Bazaar*'s Visionary Men. He also slaps on Twitter. Combining wit with serious intent, lowbrow with highbrow, he unpacks pop culture on Radio National's *Stop Everything*, and contributes journalism to media such as *The Monthly* and *Good Weekend*, and wrote a seminal *Quarterly Essay* about the undermining of Safe Schools, titled 'Moral Panic 101'.

I had every reason to be picked on at school. I was really scrawny in primary school, exactly one head size – like a human skull – shorter than my classmates. I was pretty much the only Asian kid in my year level, I didn't play sport, and was just really into reading. I should have been mercilessly bullied. But, for some reason, my classmates thought I was a cool novelty. I had a shaved head, so it felt like a soft toilet brush, and they'd rub it for luck. I had a quick wit, and the oldest students basically saw me as a mascot, barely human, more like a cartoon character really.

There were two main reasons I think I was never figured out as gay in school. One was that I'm Asian, and people can only handle a certain amount of minorities in one person. For me to be Asian *and* gay would have been taking it too far. I slipped under the radar.

The other is, when I hit puberty, my balls must have dropped like anvils or something. I suddenly developed this super-deep, baritone voice. So there was this runty, skinny Asian guy walking around sounding like James Earl Jones. I didn't have the 'voice' that a lot of people associate with gay guys.

It was the '90s, and probably the last few years where it was social suicide to come out at school. I basically knew I was gay throughout high school, maybe even before, but it was impossible to talk about what 'gay' was because it was the worst thing you could be. You couldn't talk about it without completely ostracising yourself.

At a young age, when kids aren't into gender roles, you can get away with more. At primary school I was sort of prancing around, and playing jump rope with the girls. I gradually became aware that if I was hanging around the girls too much it was seen as odd. If I said, say, I liked the TV show *Man O Man*, then I'd be told, 'Nah, you can't talk about that show. Why are you watching that?'

You don't want to be gay, right? If everyone in the schoolyard and on television is telling you that being gay is one of the most embarrassing, horrific things you could be? It's a hideous prospect. You don't want that! I was incredibly ashamed, because gays were the freaks, and the only gays you saw were when the Mardi Gras came on, and to all your friends, and even to you, they looked like an absolute freak show.

And if there's one thing that kids and teenagers are very, very efficient and good at, it's being able to smell out any sort of gayness or difference – even before the other kid knows they are gay or different. People would get up at assembly, and they'd have a slightly gay voice, and everyone would crack up laughing. Or people would call each other 'lesbo' or 'homo' or 'fag' or whatever, when someone was acting 'gay', or liked drama too much.

So you find ways of, at the very least, not acting like that. My strategy was to hide it. Not talking about it became important. You know, they say gay people are very good actors, and you have to be to survive. You see the kids who can't hide it, and how they get picked on, so I examined them and did the opposite of what they did. It was pretty dark. I watched other guys, and how they acted, and copied them. I'd see myself walking in a glass reflection, and think, 'Oh, okay, I need to take longer strides, because that's how manly men walk.'

I became super-conscious about what I wore. 'Do these pants reveal that I'm gay?'

I stopped doing gymnastics as well. For one thing it was really intensely physically painful, but it was also a prissy thing that you just rule out. I had some good friends, but I felt very cut off as a teenager. There's a level of self-consciousness that you carry constantly, a gnawing little monkey on your shoulder. It was suffocating. I questioned myself all the time, making sure I didn't emphasise the fagginess of liking books and drama.

I remember giving a Valentine's Day card to a girl who I thought *maybe* I liked. I knew I liked guys, but I thought maybe I could like girls as well. You try, but it feels wrong and strange. It just lands you in trouble, because they ask you if you like them online, and you end up fumbling and closing the window, saying goodbye really awkwardly.

You adapt. Playing a role wasn't something I consciously thought about. It's like a reflex. If the other guys are into Sarah Michelle Gellar, and think she is a babe, you pick that up straight away and start talking about Sarah Michelle Gellar as a babe. You have to put on a bit of a show, present yourself as someone you're not. I think most kids have to develop a playground persona, and for gay kids it's a lot more pronounced. Particularly in high school, when everyone talks about who they want to f**k, who they've got a crush on, and 'Did you see those tits on TV last night?' You use that vocabulary. There's a bit of bogan in me that I can switch on if I need to. I can bogan it up.

The thing that came naturally to me, which wasn't much of an act, was to be gross and disgusting. I still like to make foul jokes, and I'm obsessed with disgusting stuff, and since this is typical macho behaviour it helped me be part of the gang. I emphasised the things people liked: jokes and stories about farts and poo.

Weirdly, I liked school, probably because my home life was hard. When I was twelve my parents split up, and Mum became a single mother of five children. That was huge. It was a really dramatic thing for all us kids, and it made for a really tough environment. We saw Dad less and less, and the discussions at home were very stressful and claustrophobic. We were always looking for escape, and I really enjoyed getting up, going to school, and getting the hell out of home.

I think all teenagers have shame about something ... body shape, acne, their family, their grades. When you come down to it, shame *is* the singular teenage experience. Because I was *really* different, a lot of my energies were extended towards trying to iron out the differences and fit in.

I found my family shameful as well, because it was – what's a nice way to put it? – difficult, and hard to function within. There was nothing shiny or glamorous about my home. I went to a quite rich private school, it was co-ed Lutheran. Hardcore. Daily devotion. I'd go to my friends' houses, and their parents had functional relationships, and their crockery matched, and their Christmas tree had a singular aesthetic rather than looking like a bomb hit it. All those things made me very self-conscious and ashamed. But, yeah, being gay was the main one.

I made up my mind to come out at seventeen, just after school had finished, and before I went to university. One of the things my parents instilled in me was whenever the opportunity presented, just take it.

Going to university was a big deal for me. Not only had I never left home, but I'd lived in the same house my entire life. Starting university represented a lot of freedoms – I was going to be making brand new friends, and I didn't want to have to hide. I didn't want to have to play games and pretend that I found Sarah Michelle Gellar really hot and wanted to stick my dick in her. I didn't want to have that conversation anymore, because it is tedious and exhausting. Telling people you are gay when you meet them is exhausting enough, but it is far more tiring having a fake conversation. I'm too lazy, in the end.

Coming out is one of the most horrific things that bind gay and lesbian or transgender kids together. You're a young person who has never been able to talk about a very fundamental secret your entire life, and you have to vocalise something in your brain that has never been said out loud. It's incredibly frightening.

I came out first to my best friend, Rebecca, and I just could not stop crying, because the fear when you're revealing yourself for the very first time is completely mortifying. She was great about it. Then I told my mum. I was really emotional and scared, and I couldn't say the word and I made her guess what was wrong.

'Are you on drugs?'

'No.'

'Have you got Rebecca pregnant?'

'No.'

'Well are you gay?'

'Yes.'

Then she said one of the most f**ked up things you can say, and one of the most brilliantly consoling things you can hear as well – 'Don't be silly. There's nothing wrong with being gay. Something went wrong in the womb, that's all.'

A few friends said they suspected, because I was really into drama and arts and books, despite growing up on the Gold Coast where everyone is sporty or a surfie. My siblings were all surprised, but then you watch home videos of, you know, ridiculous fashion parades, and they start shaking their head and think, 'How did we not know?'

One by-product, I guess, of the double life, is that I learned how to please people, and make sure they see what they want to see. You know that you don't fit in, so you sort of force yourself to fit in. You find a way of making people like you. It's a stereotype, but a lot of gay men are funny, right, and I think humour is a way of getting people on side. I could make people laugh, and that took attention away from the fact that, for instance, I liked guys.

I made jokes, and hey, sometimes those jokes were gay jokes, which is weird when you think back on it. The sad thing is, I watched kids known to be gay who were picked on, and that meant you avoided them as if your life depended on it, because if you associated with them you copped flak as well. So you avoid the other kids who are gay. It makes it lonelier.

I didn't want to be ostracised, so I became very good at making sure that people were close to me. The idea was that when I eventually did come out, even though they would be shocked or horrified, they would still like me. I tried extra hard to make sure people were on side, that they weren't going to target me out. I wasn't friends with everyone at school, but I knew everyone's name in my year level, and that was a few hundred students.

Having to develop that skill at school has helped me a lot later on. I tend to gel with everyone, even if I'm an outsider. In that sense I get along no matter what background someone comes from. If you're highly educated, or an out-in-the-regions bogan, I can find common ground, because I've got both things in me.

I have good instincts, too. I chose good friends, in the end. All the high school friends I keep in contact with are open-minded, they've got a good sense of humour, they're tolerant. I wasn't adapting my behaviour to please them; I was adapting my behaviour because there was no other choice. You just didn't come out when I was at school. At all!

It took me a while to realise how different my experience was to most other people, that I had a unique perspective. My parents split up, I grew up Asian in a region where there were very few others, and I went through school hiding my sexuality. Later on I realised that writing was a good medium to start channelling a lot of those episodes of childhood/teenage horror.

And when I did start writing, I was very much hoping that someone like me was reading it, because I desperately wanted to read something like that when I was younger. There were so few representations on TV and in magazines of 'gay', and if you didn't want to be that big, Sydney, flashy sort of gay, there weren't any other templates.

I mean, look, I had a good set of friends, but there is another type of loneliness that comes with not being able to share the fundamental thing that defines you. I read a lot of Amy Tan, gravitated to her, because the Chinese experience wasn't really being written about in Australia.

I couldn't find any gay first-person stuff at all, so when I found David Sedaris in my late teens I f**king devoured him. He was growing up gay and hiding it, so I could relate to him – and he was *laughing* about it. It was mind-blowing, a revelation. Now I'm conscious, when I'm writing, of trying to talk to a younger version of myself.

When you're young you are so angsty, earnest and serious. I mean, f**k, I grew up in the '90s, when everyone was into grunge, and no one had a sense of irony. What I'm trying to write now is, 'Not only is that stuff hideous, but it's also funny.' You come out of it being able to laugh. It's a bit pep-talky. You know, 'It's okay to be a gaysian from a broken home.'

Leading a double life has fed into my writing. Something I learned about drama in writing school is that the most interesting thing you can get out of a character is what's going on with their private face versus their public face. The differences were really pronounced for me, and as a writer you look for those dual personalities in people. I always ask myself, 'What are you hiding?' You become a stickybeak.

I think everyone's an outsider. Everyone has a unique perspective, is utterly bizarre, has something that sets them apart. Sometimes I see a big burly footballer, a white hetero dude, who would have never felt like an outsider their entire life, speaking on TV for a pre-match interview. And I think, 'You know, you are one of the strangest creatures in the world.'

KATE MILLER-
HEIDKE

It's possible to imagine Queenslander Kate Miller-Heidke not fitting in, even though she's blonde, charming and luminous. Her platinum-selling, idiosyncratic songwriting tells the story, pointing to that deadly schoolyard double whammy of weapons-grade quirk and emotional sensitivity.

Being an odd little unit made school challenging for Kate but her eclecticism has worked wonders as an adult. She trained in opera and won awards as a classical singer, but pivoted to pop and writing her own material, becoming a fiercely independent artist. She represented Australia at Eurovision in 2019, swaying on a 7-metre pole as she sang her song 'Zero Gravity', and one of her most popular songs on YouTube is 'Are You F*cking Kidding Me?', a viral hit about an ex trying to 'friend' her on Facebook.

Kate's music packs an emotional punch, something she attributes directly to experiencing misery in the schoolyard. 'Caught in the Crowd', her song about school bullying and not being a bystander, remains iconic. Her most popular single, 'The Last Day on Earth', is about grief and loss.

A prolific and versatile songwriter with five studio albums, four of them top ten including 2020's *Child in Reverse*, Kate's been nominated for seventeen ARIA awards. She also co-wrote the lyrics and music for *Muriel's Wedding the Musical*, for the opera *The Rabbits*, and competed as Queen on *The Masked Singer*. Kate Miller-Heidke is unrepentantly herself, and it's just as well she didn't try too hard to fit in at school.

You know you look at a Grade 1 kid, and they're only five years old? And they look so tiny and innocent? Yet it's so important for kids to rank themselves in some kind of social structure. Within the first week of Grade 1 at primary school I was acutely aware of the social hierarchy that was going on. By week two or so, I'd ranked every kid in my grade from one to one hundred, in terms of their popularity and status. And ... I was about the fourth least popular. There were a couple of kids who had learning difficulties so I always had one up on them.

I was really sensitive, and aware of it. But at the same time I couldn't modify my own behaviour, so I couldn't figure out a way into this intricate system. The reason I graded everyone was because I was near the bottom. If you're up high there's no need. They do say that the happiest people in life are the loud, ignorant ones, and those who are quiet and introspective struggle.

The schools I went to were mainly, I guess, upper middle class. The criteria for being popular, or at least socially acceptable, were being good at sport, having symmetrical features, and not having any opinion that others might deem weird. I was shit at sport, and really eccentric.

In Grade 3, I announced to my class I was going to become a stripper when I grew up, and that pretty much destroyed my social life for the rest of primary school. I was about eight, and I don't know where I got that from. Luckily I kind of raised my standards as I grew up.

I just didn't fit in with the other kids. At the same time as being highly sensitive, I was socially weird. I still am. I had a complete paralysing insecurity coupled with completely irrational confidence, and that turned people off. I was bullied all through primary school, and through to Years 8 and 9 in high school.

When it came to sport I was picked last for every team, and you know how you had to line up and hold hands in groups of two outside the classroom? Nobody wanted to hold my hand. It sounds pitiful and stupid now, but I found it terrifying, because I knew I would end up at the back of the line by myself. That's a big thing when you're a kid.

I always felt like an outsider. I've got two brothers, but even though my younger brother was at the same schools, he was too young to be an ally. So I really felt isolated, and I couldn't talk to my parents about it because it seemed so trivial and insignificant. They can't get on the wavelength of a small child, and how devastating it is to be socially rejected when you're six or seven years old. I always remember that feeling, that I couldn't tell them because they'd just say, 'Oh, get over it,' or 'It doesn't matter.'

At high school I'd go sit in a toilet cubicle through morning tea, and all of lunchtime, so I didn't have to see anyone. There were very good acoustics in there, so I'd sing, but I'd stop if anyone came in, and wait till it was empty. I'm sure that did a lot for my reputation: 'That crazy bitch is in the toilets again.'

There was a boy who used to prick me with safety pins all through maths in Year 8, and there was one girl who took a big dislike to me, and every time I'd see her – anywhere in the school – she would run up and give me a dead leg, or a dead arm, and scream insults at me and stuff. Then one day in Year 9 she just punched me in the face.

That was that and I changed schools. I had a great excuse to leave in that my father had just become principal; obviously it becomes worse when your dad's principal. Both my parents are teachers, and all in all I changed school six times in primary school, because they got posted around different places in regional North Queensland.

I did try and fit in. In Years 8 and 9 I observed some of my popular classmates from a distance – obviously they wouldn't let me too near them – but I saw how they acted, and how they spoke, and when I changed schools in Year 10 I did an incredibly accurate impersonation of a popular kid.

It was very successful, and I was at the top of the social hierarchy for the year. Then I changed schools again because they wouldn't let me do both music and drama, and at the new school I just couldn't be bothered keeping up the charade because it was too tiring. I settled back into where I belonged.

The first friends I made were in the children's chorus of a couple of amateur musicals up in Brisbane because everybody was the reject from their school. That was a great outlet. I was in the chorus for *Oliver* twice and I still know people from then. Most of them are extremely successful now.

Things ease up for everybody around Year 11, I reckon. I became friends with the smokers and the musicians, and, yeah, we were the weird kids. I was happy with that. I felt that was my place. I had good friends for the first time in my life, and they were all artistic in some way. There weren't many, but enough. I think as long as you've got three or four friends in life you're okay.

What's great about getting older is the pressure to fit in morphs and changes into an appreciation for people who are different, and almost an admiration. I know *I* love strange people. Most of my friends are very eccentric, some of them highly eccentric, and I like those sort of people, I find them interesting.

The isolation of school can be extreme. You're surrounded by people all the time, and yet it's the loneliest place in the world if you don't fit in. But I'm grateful for it now, because it made me retreat into music, into my own brain. Being an outsider is useful, because at the heart of good songwriting is the ability to observe. That's the key: to observe, and articulate an experience in a new way.

What I've taken from being bullied is there's this little knob of self-hatred that comes in handy when it comes to being able to self-examine and self-criticise. Particularly in terms of doing drafts of your work, and knowing what to cut and to keep. It means I'm being constantly challenged to do better, and create better things, because whatever I create I still hate myself to a degree. It's a spur; maybe the next thing will help me like myself a bit more.

I'm driven by that feeling that nothing's ever good enough. There's no room for complacency. It's a useful feeling for an artist: that everything I've done in the past is shit and I have to do better next time. I'm never satisfied. And, as an artist, having a nice big well of pain and insecurity to draw on always helps. Having feelings of isolation and rejection can be handy songwriting tools. I wrote 'Caught in the Crowd' inspired by that time, and it's my favourite song off the album *Curiouser*. It resonates deeply with me, and I get a lot of young people mentioning it, saying the song helped them in some way. I'm so glad about that.

I think if you've been happy your whole life you probably don't have much to say as a songwriter. It was hard at the time, but I know for sure that I wouldn't be doing what I'm doing now, had not every element been in place – the kind of child I was, the kind of people that were at my schools. Everything has led up to this point and I don't regret any of it.

It's made me stronger; I don't feel defeated at the first hurdle. I feel like nothing's ever come easily. And doing music as a career you get a hundred setbacks for every one small success, so that's probably been useful. In that sense I'm psychologically adapted to being an artist, but that's not to say I don't have self-doubt. But I think everyone in the arts experiences that friction between complete arrogance and total self-loathing, and it's where those two overlap that great art can be made.

I feel self-sufficient as a person. I'm pretty independent and fairly resilient. As a musician you have to deal with bad reviews and people's negative opinions of what you do, and I feel like I've had a bit of practice with that. One legacy is that it's hard for me to collaborate. I collaborate with my husband [Keir Nuttall], but it took a long time to be able to trust and open up. I haven't done much with other people; I've tried and it's been quite awkward, so it's something I'd like to work at.

It's a cliché, I know, but I honestly do think being bullied was character building. Because it was impossible to express myself socially, I was basically forced to withdraw into my own head, my own imagination, and often just live in a fantasy world. I was an inherently creative child, and I'm appreciative that I had that outlet. It's nice to be good at one thing when you're a kid.

I always loved dancing, singing, musical theatre and generally making a fool of myself. That was what consoled me and comforted me growing up. I used to spend five or six hours a day in my room playing my guitar, writing songs and listening to music. I was actually really miserable, but I wouldn't swap it for anything. I'm glad, now, because I do think it leads to a much richer inner life.

I think most intelligent people at some stage in their lives have to withdraw. If you just float along in a sea of good looks and popularity all your life, and never truly have to examine what it means to be a human, well, you don't end up being an artist. One of the definite advantages of being unpopular is that you are actually forced to examine yourself.

'Caught in the Crowd'
Songwriters: Kate Miller-Heidke, Keir Nuttall.

There was a guy at my school when I was in high school
We'd ride side by side in the morning on our bicycles
Never even spoken or faced each other
But on the last hill we'd race each other

When we reached the racks, we'd each go our own way
I wasn't in his classes, I didn't know his name
When we finally got to speak, he just stared at his feet
And mumbled a sentence that ended with James

I was young and caught in the crowd
I didn't know then what I know now
I was dumb and I was proud and I'm sorry

If I could go back, do it again
I'd be someone you could call friend
Please, please believe that I'm sorry

Well, he was quite a big guy, kinda shy and quiet
When the kids called him weird, he didn't try to deny it
Every lunchtime he'd spend walking by himself
'Round the boundary of the grounds 'til he heard the bell

Well, one day I found him, joined him on his walk
We were silent for a while until we started to talk
I told him my family were fighting in court
He said his step-dad and him always fought

We talked about music, he was into punk
Told me all the bands that I liked were junk
I said I'd never heard the songs the Sex Pistols sang
I laughed back at him and then the bell rang

I was young and caught in the crowd
I didn't know then what I know now
I was dumb and I was proud and I'm sorry

If I could go back, do it again
I'd be someone you could call friend
Please, please believe that I'm sorry

It was after school in the afternoon
The corridors were crowded as we came out of the rooms
Three guys I knew pushed him into the cement
Threw away his bag and said he had no friends

He yelled that he did and he looked around
Tried getting up but they pushed him on down
That's when he saw me, called out my name
And I turned my back and just walked away
Yeah, I turned my back and just walked away

I was young and caught in the crowd
I didn't know then what I know now
I was dumb and I was proud and I'm sorry

If I could go back, do it again
I'd be someone you could call friend
Please, please believe that I'm sorry
Please, please believe that I'm sorry

HAZEM
EL MASRI

Hazem El Masri, rugby league legend and (until his record was finally surpassed in 2021) the code's greatest goal kicker, is a tough guy with a gentle heart. Growing up in war-torn Lebanon, Hazem had to harden up fast. As the eldest son he'd head out at 1am, or later – when the shooting died down – to look for bread with his father.

Hazem, nicknamed 'El Magic' during his decorated playing career with the Canterbury Bulldogs, landed in Sydney with his family when he was 12 years old. Not knowing a word of English, and small for his age, Hazem was bullied by schoolmates who mistakenly thought he'd be easy to push around. His motto is 'Never give up'.

He has spent his life making a stand: in Lebanon, at school, then as the NRL's first-ever Muslim player. Conscious that eyes were always on him, Hazem took pride in being honourable and the best, and the largest crowd ever recorded for a non-grand final turned up to his farewell game.

After retiring from first-grade rugby league in 2009, he became part of the code's One Community Ambassador Program and devoted himself to transforming lives of school kids, stamping out bullying wherever he finds it. The University of Western Sydney conferred him an Honorary Doctor of Letters in recognition of his services to the community.

Hazem takes strength from his faith, and also from his experiences. He credits his background with giving him the steel to become an elite sportsman, and says that if he hadn't been through tough times, he wouldn't be who he is today.

It was difficult arriving in Australia, not just for me but for my siblings and family. Australia was in recession, so financially it was very tough. I was twelve, so school-wise I landed in the middle of Grade 6, and it was hard, obviously, not speaking the language and trying to make new friends.

It was a shock finding myself here. But I was second oldest, the oldest of the boys, coming from a family of five, so I had to be as brave as I could and lead the way. It was always going to be difficult, seeing what my father and mum had to go through in Lebanon, trying to shield us, protect us, and make sure we had a safe environment. But in places like that you mature early, because it teaches you hardship and self-sufficiency. At a really early age you recognise these things.

We moved to Australia from Lebanon to seek a better life. My parents wanted survival for us kids. We wanted to get away from the war, and the lack of work for my dad. Dad had had to leave school when he was eleven or twelve. My grandfather, a carpenter, needed a hand, and pulled him out of school to help him in his workshop. Dad was the oldest out of eleven kids, so I mean, it's hard for me feeding two or three and they had eleven!

Dad did not want that for us. He wanted us all to go to school and finish school. Same with my mum. The older generation have always suffered for our happiness, and we take that for granted, you know what I mean? Sometimes you need to actually sit down and give them all the credit they deserve.

Of course my schooling was affected by war. Look, when it comes to war you'd have two, three months off then come back for a little bit, then more time off. People were more preoccupied with trying to survive. I got as much education as I could. Mum hired an extra teacher for after school; Dad would make sure we did our work and got an education. I always picked things up quickly.

The biggest learning curve for me, when I got here, was learning English: how to read and write and communicate with others. Massive. I was pretty fortunate, because it was a multicultural school, so coming from an Arabic-speaking background there were a couple of people who spoke my language. And I'd learned a little bit of French back in Lebanon, and it was easier to swap that around, you know what I mean? It's easier from French to English than Arabic to English. But basically I read as much as I could and I had a very good teacher, who I did my best to learn from. I did my homework. I just wanted to improve, you know? I went a couple of times a week to the intensive English stream. And I learned a lot of English once I started playing footy. You pick up the Aussie lingo properly with the footballers, I can tell you that.

I found my way eventually, but it was tough at the beginning. When I was twelve, I was still small compared to the other kids. I didn't mature until later. But the language barrier was always the toughest. Trying to express yourself when you don't know the language, and are from an obviously different background, it was always going to be difficult. Some of the bigger kids saw that as a weakness, and they wanted to intimidate me. They thought it might be funny pushing someone around. Might make them tough in front of everyone, especially their friends and the girls. So they tried to stamp their authority, show how dominant they were.

I've always had a gentle nature about me, inherited from my parents, and that's the way I wanted to be in school. But I've always stood up for myself. I never started a fight but I'd always defend myself. I hated being pushed around for no reason and being looked down upon. So I got into some altercations.

In the first couple of weeks I was playing marbles, and when I bent down to pick one up, I copped this kick in my backside. I fell down, and everybody started laughing. When I got up there was this massive kid there, laughing his head off. I was in shock, so I just stared at him, and he took that as, 'This guy wants to have a go at me.' He was used to bullying people, I guess, and them just walking away.

So I couldn't speak English, or ask him what he was doing, or explain myself. I was really angry and confused that he was making fun of me. And for no reason! It didn't make sense. But he kept pushing me around and then I pushed back. So I'm small but I'd always been strong. I take after my dad – he was always into staying fit – and when you do sport you're fit, and I played soccer back in Lebanon. I did a bit of self-defence and then he was in a headlock on the ground. He kept tapping my hand, trying to get me to stop, and they separated us and sent us to the office.

The guy was known as a big bully, and the teacher said to him, 'This is finished, right now. If you touch Hazem again you're gonna be expelled.' And then a couple of days later I see him in the park, with his cousin, who was even bigger, a monster, and this totally massive guy looks at me and says, 'You hit my cousin.' I was on my own, and I was like, 'Oh my god, I am in trouble.' And what happened was the kid stopped it. He came between me and his cousin and begged, 'Please don't touch him, if anything happens to him I'm gonna get expelled.'

I always remembered this. That it helped, reporting it to a teacher, and the teacher didn't dismiss it. In all the work I do with kids now, I always encourage them to report stuff. And I also tell them not to be bystanders, you know. Don't just watch what happens and think, 'Thank god it's not me,' because bullies thrive on encouragement and being funny, and if you just say, 'Stop it, it's not cool,' that can be enough.

Having to defend myself didn't stop. There were a couple of encounters in Grade 6, but in high school it got worse. At least when you're halfway through Grade 6 you're just being picked on by Grade 6s, or big Grade 5s. But in high school, in Year 7, I was the smallest kid there. Year 10 guys wanted to push me around because they were bigger. It happened a lot.

One Year 10 guy enjoyed slapping me in the back of the neck. The first time I said, 'Mate, can you please not do that?' But he thought it was funny so he did it again. And he was a lot bigger than me, and I didn't want to get involved. The next time he sees me he does it again and I ask him to stop. Again, he thinks it's funny. Then a third time and a fourth time ...

You know, some kids walk away from a kick and a slap. I can't do that. I like to go down swinging, as they say. I can't live my life being abused all the time. So I thought, 'That's enough. Next time, I'll get beaten up, whatever, let's get it over with, but that's enough.' So I was having fun at lunchtime with my friends and I just copped this massive slap. And honestly, I wanted to break down and cry. He's sitting there with all of his mates, thinking it's funny, and I grabbed my can of drink and threw it at him. I think it hit the ground, and he goes, 'You know what? Here's the can. Do it again if you're a man.' So I threw it again, and he charged at me, wanting to hurt me in front of his friends. A Year 10 picking on a Year 7.

He underestimated my ability. I think *I* underestimated my ability. I got hold of him on the ground and started laying into him, and they broke us up. His friends were going, 'Oh, mate, he *gave* it to you,' and he was really offended. He came up before the next lesson and said, 'I could hit you after school, but you know what, let's just call it even and then we'll walk away.' And that's all I wanted. To be left alone.

I always backed myself. I made sure I didn't just take it. I try to avoid the problem as much as I can, and I'm patient. I'll try and work it out. But when you're backed into a corner, I believe in self-defence. I've been through it so many times in my life, people picking on me for no reason, and I've had to turn the tables.

My thing has always been that I respect myself very highly, and want others to respect me. I believe respect is important. I didn't want it because I was a bully or anything, I wanted it because I was a good person that always tried to help.

I didn't spend a lot of time in the principal's office. I was a good kid, got a lot of awards. My parents were always being invited to school to see me being given awards. I had never been the aggressor: it was always me being the victim, you know? It's not, 'Oh, I had a target on my back,' but early on it happened a lot because I couldn't express myself.

My path has always been sport. Even on my first day at school, no one knew my name, and I stood there, wanting to be chosen and to play, and I was chosen last. But after playing through lunchtime – I'd been a soccer player in Lebanon – and the next day everybody wanted me on their team first. Being able to find a way through sport was fantastic, first soccer, then league.

I only played league in my last year of school. The Bulldogs just happened to put out preselectors, and I was picked up as soon as I finished, in 1994, to be part of their training squad. Early the next year, I was playing in the under 21s, and in 1996 I played first grade, so it happened very, very quickly. I watched the Bulldogs win a grand final, and the next year I was playing in that team!

I made sure I didn't rest there. I didn't succeed one year and say, 'Look, I've done it.' I was determined to leave my legacy there to show, despite my background and all the club dramas, that I performed, played more games than anybody and achieved everything I wanted. You might do it tough, you can go through adversity, but you can bounce back. That's always been my philosophy.

Being a Lebanese Muslim, I went through many difficult things. The Bali bombings and September 11, the war in Lebanon, the Sydney-based Lebanese gang rapes, the Cronulla riots, all of those affected me personally. Because I happen to be Lebanese and Muslim, and happen to be a role model. So people wanted to hear me talk about these things, even though I didn't choose to. So conflict shaped who I am today.

It's affected me enormously, more than any other player in the past decade or, even, since the game has existed. It's really tested me, obviously, coming from a war-torn country at the age of twelve, not speaking a word of English, and yet making it through to play nationally and represent Australia.

I believe God put me here to experience things, so that now I can share my story. You need to have the battle scars on you to be able to bounce back and get through to the other end. I've been down and out, but I made sure it made me stronger. It's made me resilient, more determined to succeed. My experiences have all made me a better person.

So when I sit down with a troubled kid, and they say, 'I'm getting bullied, you don't know what it's like,' I can say, 'Yes, that happened to me.' Doesn't matter what it is – 'I've been ripped off by someone,' 'I've seen people smoke bad stuff,' 'People are racist,' – and I can say, 'Yeah, I know. It's happened to me. What is it? Your background? Your religion? Your work? I've experienced it all.' And I say, thank god for that! For giving me these experiences. They were very tough but I've got the ammo to go out there and help these kids. Talking from experience makes all the difference.

I've learned that karma will always get you. If you're going to hit someone, you're gonna cop it. You might think it's funny when you're being a bully, but in reality everything will come back. I always tell the kids I speak to, 'Who's got siblings here?' and they put their hands up, and I say, 'If you see someone bully them, what do you want to do?' And I've said that at hundreds of schools and they always say, 'We'll attack them, we'll jump them, we'll bash them.' Well, you know what? If you're picking on that person, what do you think his brother or sister is gonna do to you? Always refer back to yourself.

And especially when it comes to social media. They sit behind the computer and they go at each other. You've got to remember you can't delete it. It will come back and haunt you. Later on in life you don't want to think to yourself, 'I pushed someone over the edge.' Kids that get teased and isolated and bullied, they get depression, and that can lead to suicide. You don't want to be the person responsible for that, do you?

I've learned you're always going to come across negative people, people who want you to not succeed, because of their hatred and jealousy. They don't have everything they want so they curse the whole world for it. One of the most important things is to surround yourself with the right people – the ones who want to see you up there, and who help you along the way. You have to recognise who's true and for you, and who's not.

It's okay to be afraid. When I was young, I was afraid, without a doubt. Even now. Some people might say being afraid is a sign of weakness but it's not. Sometimes it's good. I'm always afraid for other people's wellbeing, for my family, my kids. But my attitude has always been, when your back's to the wall, when you're afraid, that's when you go all out.

I'm not afraid of that, because I've got faith in my God, in myself, in my community, in my family. I'm a human being and I've made stupid decisions, but when I do fail I make sure I learn from that mistake. My faith has helped me be stronger, for sure. One hundred per cent. My faith in God has played a major role in my life. It's not a public thing, but it's what shapes me, drives me, and is behind the decisions that I make.

I consider myself extremely lucky to come from a war-torn country and now be in Australia. I have a good life with my family, and good people around me. I love what I do, I love my job and I can't speak highly enough of it. I travel all over the country with the NRL, and I spread the same message: if you do good, karma will bring it back. Above all I try to teach people, especially students, to believe in themselves and work hard.

My community gets a lot of bad publicity being Muslims and Lebanese. I was on a fundraiser for Channel 9 trying to help raise some money, answering the phones, and one of the callers, she's like 'Hello, who am I talking to?' and I told her who I was, that I played with the Bulldogs and all that, and she said, 'Oh yeah, you're the good Muslim!' I just started laughing and I said, 'Yeah, thank you. You know, we're not all the same – I know what you might have heard.'

I'm only one of many Muslims and Lebanese who go out there and do a lot of good work but, for me, it just shows my good work has been paying off, you know. People get to recognise there is good work, and good people, in all different cultures and religions.

KAREN FROM
FINANCE

Karen from Finance, the alter ego of performer Richard Chadwick, is one of Australia's most recognisable and beloved character drag queens. She's known for her kind, mothering vibe, her work ethic, her community-building, her raucous office-themed schtick and her sharp wit. Karen has built an international career, starring in *Death Drop*, a UK drag-based murder-mystery stage play, in 2021. She was a finalist in the first antipodean outing for RuPaul's iconic reality TV franchise, *RuPaul's Drag Race Down Under*, and *Out of Office*, her debut solo comedy show, won awards and toured Australia for four years. Karen's raison d'être is to bring people happiness.

But Karen wouldn't exist if Richard hadn't been nursing secret pain from childhood. A sunny, sensitive kid, Richard learned to mask his grief from the age of four when his mother was diagnosed with breast cancer. She died when he was fourteen – a cataclysm for Richard, his two younger brothers and his father. Richard spun off from his religious school into a trajectory of rebellion and self-questioning, and reinvented himself with a heteronormative, emo, Jim Beam–drinking, straight-talking persona to hide his queerness and survive adolescence. It's been a long journey from 'masking for his life' to radical authenticity as Karen from Finance – and the loss of his mother is perennial – but Richard is wiser for the grief, and draws on the skills and techniques he developed every day, delighted that his powers for reinvention allow him to spread joy.

I have beautiful memories of my childhood. Both my parents were around, and my brothers and I were very happy kids. It was a different time: we played outside a lot, riding bikes in the night and living the dream! I grew up in Hallam, in the south-east of Melbourne, and went to a Catholic private school in Dandenong. I was good at school, a bit of a teacher's pet, and I had lots of friends. I tried sports – basketball, football, tennis, cricket, swimming – but I hated them all equally. Mum and Dad realised I wasn't interested, so when I was in Grade 4, they let me enrol in the Helen O'Grady Drama Academy in Cranbourne, and it was life-shaping. My childhood was really cool. That's still how I remember it.

But in the background, my mum had breast cancer. She was diagnosed when I was four and I grew up with her being very sick. We never knew anything else and it's incredible, really, that they were able to raise us to be happy. There were a couple of years where we celebrated, thinking the cancer had gone, and she had another baby – my brother Andrew – but then it came back to stay. For the final three years, Mum lived in hospital what seemed like full-time, having chemo and radiation treatment, and she passed away when I was fourteen. She was 37. So young. It was horrible.

Those last few years were hard and tough and weird. We'd go to school, go to the hospital, go home, do homework from 9pm and not get much sleep. We were being trained to understand what it was like not to have her around the house, having her in and out of hospital for such a large chunk of time. We started grieving long before she passed. But when she did it was still a slap in the face. We'd been happy, still, while she was around, but for a few years after that things got really, really dark.

I think it's fair to say I was the closest to my mum. We were very close. I loved the female energy she and her friends gave me, and I went to her for that. It resonated with me. My brothers were rough and sporty and I was soft and gentle. I'm told now – as an adult – that Mum acknowledged I was going to be gay from when I was as young as two. I had felt that way from kind of before I could remember. I thought it was normal.

When Mum died, I was overwhelmed with loneliness. It felt like I was the only one left. The whole family felt that way, I think. It was all incredibly isolating. Everyone shut off. We all shut off from the outside and we shut off from each other. We stopped relying on each other.

My dad responded by moving on quickly to a new relationship. There was no warning, and he moved her in within weeks. I absolutely understand now that it was his way of coping, of dealing with his grief, but it was incredibly confronting. Our extended family didn't agree with it, so Dad pushed them away, and we went from having a large, loving family and lots of support to having no one. She had three kids, too, with custody on weekends, so from Friday to Sunday there were six of us kids and the two parents in a small house.

Everything changed. The family unit became sad and depressing. Suddenly we all began to look forward to the weekend, because during the week it was just us at home, and on the weekend, we could get away. Being away from the family became a breath of fresh air.

My brothers and I had been very close but that stopped. They became even sportier and Dad picked up football as well. So, between the three of them, in one week there would be three matches, six sets of training and a match report on Sunday night. It was an overpowering amount of sport. That's, like, more than three football events a day – or at least it felt that way. It became the three footy boys and little old me.

When I was older, before I moved out, I was music-obsessed and wanted to see shows all the time. There was one band, Little Birdy, that I really loved. They were on tour, and I was flying to see them in every city they played. Just before dinner one night, my dad said, 'Ah, don't you get sick of that? It's so repetitive. It's just the same thing over and over again.' And I thought, 'How dare you? You play football every day!' It was pivotal. I'd never felt less understood.

I'm sure I was awful back to Dad, though. My personality and outlook had changed. When Mum passed, it became clear that things don't stay the way they'll always be. Not everyone gets to grow old together. I understood my future was up to me and I snapped out and broke away quickly. I really changed *everything*. I became rebellious, I turned into a 'nasty' kid at school – to an extent. I didn't stop being *good* at school but I stopped caring. I became a punk emo, classic black clothes and dyed hair. I went out drinking. I got work at KFC and threw everything I had into it. I've always been a workhorse, and even in a crappy job I wasn't interested in one three-hour shift a week; I wanted full-time straight away. I wanted purpose, acceptance, anywhere to hide the loneliness.

My job at KFC was one of the first times I 'took on' a role: the performance of being happy when I wasn't. I started to do it in everything – in my social networks, my friendship circles, at school. I also moved schools for my final year to be with my new friends from KFC. Big change. It was a state school, ranked in the top-ten worst state schools in Victoria. It was easy to be, you know, top of the class there, but I could express myself. They had a uniform, but it was lax. I could dye my hair and get my ears pierced and wear sneakers.

The Catholic private school had been very regimented and strict. It was all about wearing your blazer and your uniform correctly, going to church, praying every day. And it was cookie-cutter vanilla. That's what they were churning out. There was a lot of pressure to conform. If you didn't have an exact plan for university, they couldn't care less about you. At the state school, if they could keep you off the street, they were happy. I'd been an altar boy but was always anti-religion. It was Mum who was religious. While she was dying, I questioned God and religion in RE, but whenever I asked anything, the teachers silenced me and gave me detention. That put religion to bed for me.

I did what I needed to in order to survive at the Catholic school. It was a *big* school: all up, from Years 7 to 12, there were about one thousand students. I was friends with everybody. I really did know them all, from the cool kids to the nerdy kids. I had friends to sit with at lunch and in class, to come over and play, or to go to the movies with. And we all had a great time. But none of them were tight friendships. I was a chameleon. I could be academic and good in class, or boisterous and rebellious and muck around with the other kids too. I could slip into any scenario. It was the performative side of me again, playing a role. In hindsight, with Mum always being sick, I think it was about controlling loss. I was keeping myself safe and my options open. I always remained neutral. Never burn any bridges: that's probably my motto to this day.

When Mum died, it was a kick up the butt to work out who I was. I'd been doing well but I didn't know what I wanted. I was kind of into law, and I was into literature. The trajectory was towards university but I rebelled. I had to find out who I was going to be, and the school had *very* specific thoughts about how I should do that. No, I don't want a clean-cut hairstyle, and to study law. I want to have a jet-black fringe, new friends, and to listen to rock-and-roll.

So in Year 12 at the state school, I was the new kid on the block, and I could reinvent myself in any way I chose. It did me wonders. I basked in that freedom, and in being able to distract from the darkness on the inside by being unique and outrageous on the outside. I'd created those techniques early on, to suppress thoughts, emotions and feelings, and the person that I was becoming. The masking, the performative heterosexuality, the hiding inside an alternative culture – I was determined to be accepted. I had no plan other than to just get by.

I knew I was going to be queer, but only subconsciously. I suppressed it and didn't acknowledge it – it was never *cognitively* there. Mum dying really was horrible – I still think about it every day – and I'd suffered enough. I had no interest in going through what I could see for my future if I leaned into being a gay person early on. There was one openly gay guy I worked with at KFC. For years, he was like, 'Oh, go on, come out, come out,' and I was like, 'How dare you even think that?' I just couldn't.

My interests were very heteronormative, so it was easy to use that to my advantage, to slip into them and tweak them a bit to cover up. Music was really important. I was obsessed with Silverchair and I loved everything they did. I was the freak in their song 'Freak', and the anorexia in 'Ana's Song' felt like Mum's cancer. Silverchair were my everything. But the rest was just terrible emo post-punk bands. Oh god. Hawthorne Heights, Mudvayne. Don't look them up! Taking Back Sunday, The Used, The Amity Affliction. Oh my gosh.

There was nothing better than a Saturday night where we could sit in the garage together and blare this music, standing in a circle and jumping around. A couple of cans of Jim Beam, some dirty cigarettes and some gross rock-and-roll! Coming home in the morning after standing around a bonfire all night! I deeply loved it at the time. I really did. There was still a lot that was genuine in the masking days.

I used what I had to mask. I used relationships, I used music, I used alcohol, I used parties. It was pragmatic. Everything was about creating this crazy, unruly, punky character that was fun to hang out with. But no one got to get too close. No one got to know me. I had a girlfriend throughout Year 12, maybe for the better part of my final year of school, and it was just about music and drinking and partying and KFC. When we hung out, we never talked about my mum dying. People got to meet my family, but we never talked about how I felt about my dad and my brothers.

With acting straight, with dating, what I thought was, 'If I engage with this, two things are going to happen. One: I'm going to experience something new in a way that will really help me decide, to suss myself out. And two: what if I could make it work; what if I could find a way to enjoy it or go with it? Then people would have no idea that I could be any other way.'

But I was always uncomfortable. People aren't clothes that I can put on and off, or a box of hair dye I can wash out. These were people with feelings. I'd hate the idea of anyone ever thinking they were used. It wasn't like that. I was using the circumstances, totally, and aspects of relationships, but it always meant more. I was hurting on the inside and hurting on my own, but I was really good at not just performing happy, but *being* happy in those moments. At home listening to my punk rock I was sad and depressed, but out with friends I was living the dream. It was just a very strange time. I think what worked is that everyone was experimenting in their own way. We had one of those friendship circles where everyone was dating everyone, and we were all trying to find ourselves.

I wasn't looking for lifelong engagements. I wasn't thinking, 'These people, they'll be my network forever, and this will be who I am forever.' Life is temporary. I was going to keep moving. But it wasn't about greener grasses, or people I thought were 'better'. I just needed new and different. A lot of us are friends on social media now. They follow me on Facebook, and some have been to shows and say congrats afterwards. My girlfriend from high school even came to the viewing party for the first episode of *Drag Race*.

I didn't consciously suppress being gay for long – only for a couple of years. Once school was over, I got through the summer, gave myself time to turn 18 and come of age, and go out and experience the world a little. And then I was like, yeah, this is inevitable now, there's no going back. Coming out was terrifying, but it's me who made it difficult – it was hard finding the confidence to have the conversations! My family responded well. The guy at KFC was like, 'I f**king knew it'. We became friends and had a lovely old time for a couple of years, hanging out, going clubbing and seeing shows.

It was so freeing but I had a lot of internalised homophobia. I wasn't proud of being gay. I didn't want to be associated with the gay community, or the stereotypical gay man. It was only when I started doing drag that I understood that the community is huge and important, and it's what you make of it. I didn't intend to do drag, either, but it became my way in. Friends and I once bought gaudy old 80s prom dresses from a thrift shop to wear to a party, and it was fun. At first, that's all Karen from Finance was to me – a means to be outrageous and nothing more. It was wild creating an office worker as a drag character, because when she did something outrageous, it was *doubly* outrageous. But that got old pretty quickly, and I developed a love for her. I wanted to know what else she could do, and as Karen developed, I changed her purpose.

The scene was *really* new to me when I started. I didn't have a network of friends who did drag. But I found a community of performers doing work that aligned with mine, and from there I was able to navigate the scene. My approach is very left of centre compared to most drag queens. Many of them see drag as an extension of themselves, their femininity, which is wonderful. But Karen's different. She's a character with a backstory, a performance, and I'm not completely in control of her. She has a life of her own and does what she wants to do. And she's become an absolute vessel for empowerment and happiness. She is sweet and loving, and I love assisting her to make people laugh, to help people feel empowered.

Karen is quite maternal. People pointed that out for a while, and I struggled to acknowledge it. But I can absolutely see it now. RuPaul told me that Karen was *my* mum but that's not right. Karen *is* a motherly figure, though. Originally, I made her unnaturally, bizarrely curvy, but I fine-tuned her shape, and now she's womanly – yes, motherly, which is just so lovely. She's very sweet and approachable. She's kind, and that's coming out more and more. There's a lot of love there, and I lean into it.

Because I approached the scene sideways, I didn't align with the shade-throwing and the bitchiness embedded in the drag community. I don't get a kick out of it and I don't enjoy it. On *Drag Race* they over-produced that aspect and I stepped back even more. It's not necessary and it's not a good example. My experience of the community is that it's supportive. In my network of performers, we lift each other up. We weren't given a platform to show that side. Karen's about creating community, and a level playing field. I feel privileged that I can offer and create that space for community, for anyone.

Dolly Parton is in Karen, too, big time. She's not a mother, but she's very maternal. She's an absolute optimist, she's a businesswoman, she's outrageous, but she's very sweet. The only thing we don't share is the godliness! In the USA, they call Dolly 'the grand unifier', which I also resonate with. It's a real gift to be able to bring people together, to create spaces where ideals can be left at the door and people can just get along.

In the current structures of Australian society, as a man there are barely any avenues for offering that sort of energy. The only way, really, is to construct special friendship circles where you can offer that to each other. It's why I jumped circles so much as a teen, trying to find that. I don't keep in touch with people from when I was younger, but I've got friends now that I've had for ten years. I've settled in and found myself. And I've developed a character where I'm authentic, and can offer that energy. I'm so happy to offer something that's so needed. Especially now, goodness me.

I developed and implemented so many strategies to get me through tough times, but I love having those skills. I use them all the time. They've helped me navigate a broad range of business opportunities and people. I absolutely have the gift of the gab, and I'm really good at socialising and networking. I'm innovative. I'm able to keep my fingers in different pies at any one time. My commitment to work is so strong because it's another way I can mitigate the possibility of loss. I throw myself into something to make sure I don't lose it.

Music's been the one constant. I love it still. My taste has changed, but the escapism that music offers is one of the most exciting things about life. I regret that I'm not a better singer – I'm really not very good! Luckily, lip-synching offers me storytelling through music, and I connect that way. And I get a real kick out of performing in venues where I used to see bands play when I was younger. I always think that's really cool.

I have an innate understanding, I think, of what it's like to live alone in your head. Some people can be on their own and not be lonely at all. And some people can be around hundreds or thousands of people and be totally alone. I have a pretty strong understanding of what that's like.

After I do my shows, I go to the merch desk or the bar for a little meet and greet. But then I love to stick around even longer, because that way you whittle an audience down from 100 people to 20, and then to just one or two, and you end up having the most beautiful conversations. It's like that conversation has made the whole day worthwhile. Making those connections is really special.

I do wish I could have been less resentful, after Mum died, towards my immediate family. I wish I could have maintained those relationships better, that I could have stepped outside how *I* was feeling to understand how *they* were feeling. But I don't know whether that was possible. I was fourteen, an angsty teenager and resentful that I wasn't everybody's number-one priority. I've been working on those relationships for a while now, and they're getting better. We're all much older. We've grown a lot. I understand that with that kind of that trauma, everyone grieves in their own way.

A few years ago, the time ticked over to where I had been alive for longer without Mum for longer than I'd been with her before she died. That was a moment of real reflection, on how wonderful she was and on how much I probably still miss her. The coming milestone will be where I'm the age she was when she died. Milestones are important. My younger brother started having his own kids a couple of years ago, and that was pivotal for our family. Watching those kids playing with each other and remembering that with your own siblings was an eye-opener in comparison to how disconnected you are as adults. It really drew us to reconnect and brought the family back together. It's allowed us to start letting each other in again.

I don't think Australians are very good at dealing with grief or talking about it. I'm good at talking about it now because I've experienced it. Sometimes I play with it a little bit, make a joke every now and then. If someone asks about my mum, I'll say, 'She's dead,' quite bluntly. I enjoy the shock. It's not because I'm dark or don't care, it's because I find it really strange that Westerners just won't talk about death.

They don't know how to offer support, either. No one knew how to manage my loss at the time. Not my school, not my dad. It would have been really beneficial if I'd been, say, buddied up with another student who'd lost a parent. After Mum died, the year-level coordinator at the Catholic school told me that five of my friends had spoken to her and they all agreed that I should go to counselling. I was like, 'What? I don't need counselling.' It felt unsupportive, like it was a jab at me – although, in hindsight, it wasn't. But it was the only approach I got and it made me feel more alone.

The best way to process anything is by communicating. It's always a journey, and the next step for me is to get into that with my family, to try to understand their grief and loss. I've always known we need to talk about it, but only subconsciously, similar to how I felt about being gay when I was younger. It's the best way forward for all of us.

CHRISTOS
TSIOLKAS
EUROPE

Christos Tsiolkas, from a Greek immigrant family, gay, working class, and intellectually curious, could give a masterclass about not fitting in. Now celebrated as one of Australia's most important, ambitious and provocative authors, Christos had an achingly lonely adolescence at a suburban monocultural high school in the late 1970s. Homosexuality was still illegal, Christianity preached he was going to hell, he was the only 'wog' at the school, and he detested sport. Christos spent a lot of time in his own company.

As a writer, Christos still draws on his teenage experiences, particularly the emotional punch of shame and isolation. One novel, *Barracuda*, is about an aspiring Olympian, who is gay, ethnic, working class, and out of his depth at an exclusive private school.

Christos is known for his powerful, transgressive writing. *The Slap*, his blockbuster novel and ABC1 TV series, is about a multicultural community that unravels when a child is slapped at a BBQ; *Loaded*, later made into the film *Head On*, focuses on a young gay man caught between his Greek upbringing and the hedonism of contemporary Australia. His most recent, *Damascus*, is based around the gospels and letters of St Paul, reimagining the time after Christ as cruel and violent, and Paul of Tarsus as a repressed gay man.

Christos escaped into reading, writing and cinema at school, hiding within his imagination and rich fantasy world. He's certain that without those endless solitary hours, a career as a writer would have remained a dream.

When I think back on my primary school years, it was a charmed existence. Everyone's parents worked in the same factories, and the factories were within a kilometre radius, so you knew everyone. We felt quite safe to go in and out of people's houses. We were all immigrant kids, so my best friends were Harry who was Greek, Victor who was Spanish, Zolati who was Yugoslav. All my memories of that Richmond period are outside; we played in the alleys and on the road. It was like we possessed the streets.

Then our family moved to Box Hill North. I was just shy of thirteen, middle of Year 8, and even though it was the same city, it was like I'd entered another Australia. I still remember the shock of walking into the classroom and seeing a sea of blonde people.

My parents moved because they wanted a bigger house, a bedroom each for their two sons. The inner city was seen as quite rough then, and their friends were moving away. I remember my dad shaking: he was so upset after a parent–teacher interview. One of my brother's teachers had said to him, 'Why are you worried about John's education? He's just going to end up in a factory.' That was the expectation. So there was an element of, 'Let's get our kids to the suburbs where there are more opportunities.'

My new school was immediately isolating. I mean, obviously I'd heard the word 'wog', and heard it used against my parents and myself, but when we were in Richmond, and we were all wogs, we were protected against the ferocity of the word. But in the first week, these three boys ganged up on me, and I remember walking past them in the corridor, them holding their noses and talking about how wogs stink.

All the rules had suddenly changed. They picked a fight, and I'm not a fighter, I never have been, and there were three against one. I remember thinking, 'Oh well, I'd better go for it,' and biting one of them, and him yelling, 'What are you doing? You're not allowed to bite,' and I realised I didn't even know how to fight correctly.

The bell would go for recess and lunch, and the kids would form their tribes and groups, and I didn't have anyone. So I would just go to the back of the oval and walk around and around and get lost in a fantasy world. I was anywhere but suburban Blackburn. I was making up worlds and dreaming of being someone else. I was making movies in my head. I would say there were two years where, if I wasn't thinking about sex, I was thinking about making movies.

I don't want to overstate the racism, because in lots of ways it was quite casual, but it was venomous. Those daily slurs were powerful. I became acutely aware of my difference. I was just becoming aware that my sexuality was – in the eyes of the world back then – abnormal, and it all came to a head. I felt like I was completely abnormal. Some weird ... thing.

For a boy back then, sport was one of the things that defined you, and because I was late to the school and a wog, I was always chosen last for teams. It became a symbol of where I sat in the hierarchy. It was a ritual of humiliation. I hated PE. Loathed it. I'd use any excuse to get out of it.

And I hated it because you had to strip, every time. I hated the showers. I'd started developing early, so I already had pubic hair and the rest, and they'd taunt me, 'Greeks are so hairy.' Stupid stuff. So I became self-conscious and disassociated from my body. I saw it as smelly, as hairy, as something disgusting. That took a long time to overcome, and even now, no matter how hard I try and fight it, I still associate physical perfection with a smooth white body.

The PE teachers were real arseholes in the late 1970s. They didn't intervene; they made it worse. You could see the contempt in their faces for kids who weren't physically able, or excluded, and they'd literally say things like, 'Don't be a cry baby.' There were some kids, physically weaker than me, who were bullied terribly, and PE class was a form of torture. The teachers did nothing.

I thought I was the ugliest kid in school. School takes up so much of your time and space so those slights accumulate and you take them on. You think you're ugly, you think you're just a weak, unlovable being. I'd wonder, 'How am I gonna kill myself?' That to me was such a part of adolescence. Sitting for hours in my room at night thinking, 'If I was to do it how would I do it?' I decided I'd be behind the wheel of a car and just drive as fast as I could into a wall. That was the fantasy, something spectacular.

The first person at the school who was friendly to me, actually kind to me, belonged to this evangelical Christian sect. I realise now there was an element of her wanting to convert people. She introduced me to J.R.R. Tolkien, who I'd never read, and after I finished *The Lord of the*

Rings she showed me the Christian analogies in the book and started inviting me to her church group.

I grew up Greek Orthodox but very anti-clerical, and feeling so isolated I just jumped into that Christian world. It was a way of battling my sexual demons. And I saw them as demons – I did not want to be gay. I had no idea how you could possibly survive it. It was impossible during that period to think I could reconcile my masculinity and my sexuality.

You know, back then, it was still illegal to be gay? It wasn't talked about and if you heard anything, it was in the most derogatory terms. For the longest time I felt I had to hide myself, live that aspect in silence. And I knew about my sexuality very, very early on. I was conscious that I was different at five or six. So I tried desperately hard to be Christian. Really hard.

It was that summer between Year 9 and Year 10, and I was so ashamed of the body I was in, that I was badly hurting myself. I remember being in bed and having these sexual fantasies, and to stop myself masturbating I'd scratch and scratch my body until I made myself bleed. Poor mum. She had these bloody sheets to deal with.

Of course I couldn't talk about it with my parents. I just kept saying to God, 'If you stop making me gay, I will do whatever you want.' In the end, I just couldn't come at it. There came a point, in one of the Pentecostal bible study groups, that they started talking about the evil of books and the evil of film and, look, I'm not even sure which writer they were talking about, but they were talking about a writer I loved, and I got up and walked out and kept going.

I just remember realising, 'Oh, there is no God.' So whatever was going to happen, there would be no 'God' to save me from what my life was. Weirdly, that was liberating. I mean, it didn't necessarily change anything about my school years but, interestingly, it was only after that realisation that I began to form firm friendships, though all of them were with girls.

Being at a co-ed school saved me. I found close relationships with the girls and I treasured those friendships. They kind of protected me from the boys, all the way through. I grew up in a time where you were either one of the boys – the jocks – or if you had an intellectual curiosity, you were a pansy or a freak. Even though the high school had a music program, there was a hostility to humanities. You were meant to do sports and be incredibly physical, and if you did really well in my favourite subjects – Art and English – well, that made you a poofter. If you like reading you're a poofter, if you like art you're a poofter. With the girls there was a safe space where you could be that. I found the girls' world fascinating, but I'm not romantic about women's friendships – I saw how girls could treat other girls. To be honest, I'd find it unimaginable to not go to a co-ed school; I'd be terrified to be with just boys all the time. I only had one male friend and eventually he turned out to be gay as well.

The path out, in the end, was books and cinema. The books I was reading and the films I was watching were like a light going on. They presented a seductive alternative and I knew there was a big world out there. I read all the time. I don't remember when I first awoke to the pleasure of reading but we're talking back in primary school. I wanted to write from very early on but I didn't know how. Coming from a very typical migrant working class life, the idea of writing as a career had a fantastical element to it, and that continued well into my adulthood.

I remember in Year 9 my teacher, Mrs Crabtree, standing in front of the class in English and tearing up my story. She said, 'This is by Chris ...' she could never pronounce my name right '... ti-ol-ka', and then she ripped it up in front of everyone. She said, 'He writes filth.' My first critic, and they haven't changed! You don't do that to a kid in Year 9. I was a very promiscuous reader, and I'd been reading a lot of Philip Roth, things like *Portnoy's Complaint* and *Goodbye, Columbus*. I was probably just writing what I was reading – I'm sure it was very derivative and not very good. It may have involved masturbation or the word 'f**k'. Back then that was enough to cause trouble.

There was maybe an element of deliberate provocation involved in writing that story, an aspect of, 'How am I not going to end up with just this? With these people being the rest of my life? How am I going to get out?' Perhaps I wanted it torn up. It's difficult to be definitive, because that time is such a confused maelstrom of emotions and hormones and fears, but the only skill I had was the skill of the imagination, so I think there's a self-styling that went on. A few years on I would probably have been a goth.

I would do people's homework for them, actually, to get liked. It was one of my strategies. I was really good at essays, so some of the kids who weren't doing well, including some of the boys who hated me because I was a 'wog' and a 'poofter', would come to me because I could write their assignments. I had currency. It didn't make me more popular, of course, but it meant that I could negotiate, and that's all I really wanted at that stage – to be in my own world and not have to engage with any of them.

By the end of school there were only ten of us in my art class. I just used to live for those classes. All of us were outsiders, one way or the other, and it was the space where we discussed feminism and sexuality and movies. That's where I found my tribe. My life got a bit easier after Year 10 because the coterie of boys that were just cruel, who'd made the walk to school and the walk back so hard, most of them left for the tech school down the road. I was so glad about that, having them out of my life.

What I remember of high school is loneliness. The time went so slowly and the aching was so deep. School seemed never-ending. My friendships with the girls were literally lifesavers. But part of loneliness is that you can't speak your truth to anyone and there were aspects of my emotional life that I was terrified of revealing to my girlfriends. So there was just a longing, I think, for a male best friend. Someone who you could share something with about who you are and what you're experiencing.

I was leading a double life, basically. I'd started experimenting with sex since I was like fifteen, and it was always with older men, because I felt that if I revealed myself to anyone at school, I'd be ostracised. I had one sexual relationship with a boy who was in the class above me. We'd gone to a party, and coming back we'd got onto the subject of David Bowie. Now, I loved David Bowie but basically 'David Bowie' was code for 'I'm bisexual'. That relationship lasted a little while. So there'd be a Chris Tsiolkas at school, and then a sexual being that was completely unknown to his friends and family. I wasn't knowable back then. I was just so careful, because I didn't want to be attacked, or undermined, or threatened, or to do the wrong thing, or be found out.

What was bizarre was that the boys thought I knew all about straight sex because I was a wog. In Year 9, right, this kid came and up and said, 'How do you get a prostitute? We know that when you're fifteen, Greek fathers take their sons to prostitutes.' Which, for the record, doesn't happen, but I ended up almost, like, studying sex because that knowledge seemed to give me kudos. I remember one of toughest kids took me aside and asked about protection. It was a very strange moment, but because I'd read about it, I could tell him.

In terms of my development, the most important moment wasn't something that happened to me, it was something I witnessed. There was one boy, Martin, who was a very gangly, clumsy, physically awkward kid. He wasn't smart either and the teachers would humiliate him publicly in front of the class. The boys would bully him physically, and the girls teased him mercilessly about how ugly he was. He spat, he had a stutter, but he loved birds, just loved them, and because the oval was my escape I'd see him out there too, making bird sounds. Talking to the birds.

And one day, at the end of Year 8, these boys went out with slingshots. They killed all these birds and stuffed them in Martin's locker. So the poor kid opens it, and these maggies and sparrows fall out, and he loses it, goes ballistic, just howling and howling. I wasn't laughing, I wasn't teasing, I was with a group who were obviously shaken by it but we didn't intervene. That is still one of the most shaming occasions of my life.

I'm still ashamed by that moment. I knew that what was happening was ... I'm gonna use the word 'evil' because I can't think of anything else. I knew in my gut what that boy was experiencing and I wasn't brave enough to do anything about it. You know you can't make excuses for it, you know that the right thing to do is stand up. But there's a pecking order, and if you befriend this person, you'll be bullied yourself. So we stayed silent. And no matter how much you pretend that that's not acquiescence, you know it is.

That moment impacted on me as a man, and as a storyteller. The 'taken-for-grantedness' of that kind of cruelty has shaped some of the ways I see the world. As I've got older, I believe you've got to speak up. You can't remain silent when you see such evidence of inhumanity. And now I write about those moments, when people don't have the courage to follow their moral convictions. It taught me something about human failure and it was a really important lesson to learn. In terms of my writing, that emotion of shame comes up again and again, about how sometimes we fail ourselves and others in what we do.

I also think those long periods of being on my own were crucial. Walking around and around and around the oval. And I'd just beat a ball against a wall, you know, for hours. What that did was exercise my imagination. Those hours were part of my training to be a writer. Certainly I had an obsession with the desire to write, to be an artist. But those long hours alone were the path that led me there. Spending so much time on my own meant that I created a sense of myself and, really importantly, I'm not scared of not being around other people. It doesn't terrify me, it doesn't make me anxious and, because my mind was so active, it actually became pleasurable for me. There is something about being alone that I really, really love.

It's interesting but because the fantasy world I created for myself was a place I felt safe, I've been able to learn to be comfortable with saying, 'I don't have to please everyone.' Unfortunately, I think one of the ways I tried to fight people's contempt or dislike was trying to be nice. It was part of the way I coped, and it's taken a long time to try and unlearn. Whenever I see a prison film I know exactly who I am. I'd be offering people cigarettes and blow jobs. It sounds like such an extreme metaphor, but school really was like being in a prison. I'd just go, 'Alright, can I make it through this day without being picked on? Without someone commenting on me?' Writing is an escape from that. I'm not nice there. I can be brave in my writing.

I always feel like a bit of traitor to my class by becoming educated, by being artistic. But those working class boys made it quite clear that I didn't fit there either. If I'd finished high school in Richmond, I'd maybe feel a greater possession around a working-class identity but the fact is I'd still have been an outsider because of my sexuality. I would have had to wrench myself away anyway. As it was, I moved out of home at eighteen to pursue the life I wanted. My parents were distraught because that wasn't what you did, but I couldn't be the good Greek kid and stay home until I got married. I loved my parents dearly, but there was no way that I could live the life I wanted to live and be in their home.

I'm actually grateful that I never felt quite at home now. I met my partner, Wayne, when I was nineteen, and we've been together ever since. So I got my best male friend. But I would never have met him if I hadn't had to get out of where I was.

As a writer I can't separate the influence of my experiences from school, the writers that made an impression on me, and cinema. They were all equally important. That world of the suburbs that I experienced also had a big part to play; it's very strongly part of the Australian environment. As, for that matter, was my desire to run away from it as fast as I could.

I think that being an outsider gives you the beginning of empathy. If you're feeling this way, if you're so isolated, if the world's not working for you, well, maybe it's not working for someone else? Maybe they're not a freak or a loser. Maybe they're also going through shit that is meaningful and important. This was another good lesson.

It's very difficult to imagine that artists can be made without the experience of not fitting in. It's part of what allows you to see beyond yourself. There must be an element of saying, 'I can see the world from another character.' And to make that claim, to observe, you have to have been outside.

But that experience, no matter how difficult the living through of it was, is something I am completely grateful for. Because it gave me an appetite to begin to explore what was outside the worlds I knew. Outside the migrant family world but also the world of suburban Australia. I was so hungry that there had to be more.

My relationship to the world is so very different to most people. I'll sometimes be at the dentist or the doctor's and there's the *Women's Weekly* or *New Idea* or *Sports Illustrated* and I'm looking at these people going, who are they? In a sense the 'real world' seems so weird, I have no relationship to that anymore. I live in the world I've created and that is more than okay.

CARLY FINDLAY

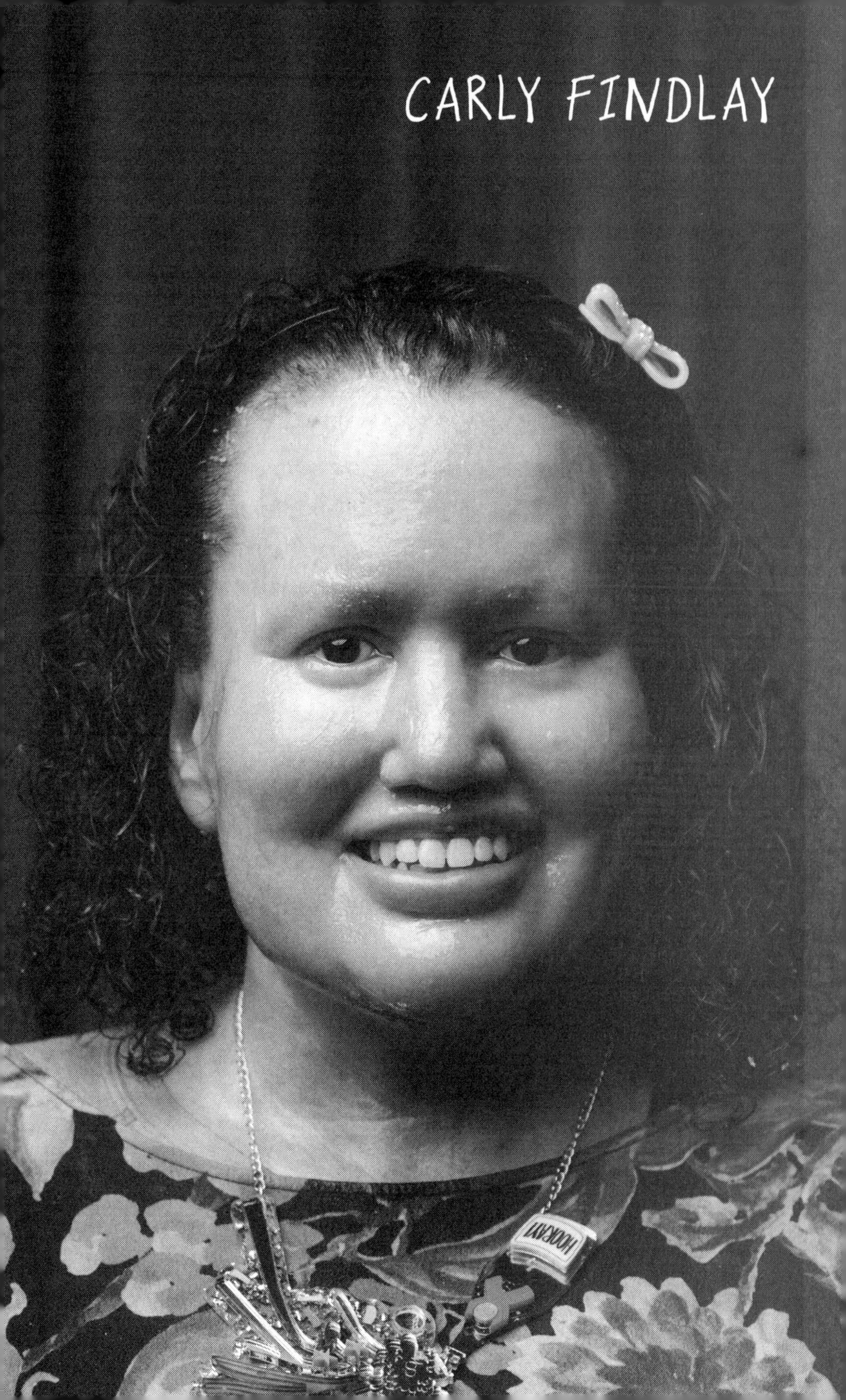

Carly Findlay, OAM – appearance activist, disability activist, writer, blogger, author, speaker and editor – is a powerful advocate and staunch challenger of discrimination and ableism via her hundred thousand-strong social media following. She is also known for her appearance on the ABC show *You Can't Ask That*, her bestselling memoir *Say Hello* and – always – her deep and abiding love for the artists Savage Garden and Bob Evans.

Carly was born with the rare and painful genetic skin disorder ichthyosis, and her skin, hospitalisations and treatments ensured she always stood out. Cruelly shunned throughout school, Carly longed for friends, acceptance and to blend in, but she later found a place online and blogged her way to confidence, pride and a kick-arse media career fuelled by her appearance activism. These days Carly's appearance *is* her brand, and she dresses to represent – in bright, joyful clothes that make her 'feel f**king fabulous'. As a kid she complained when she was bullied, and now she stands up for her communities. She demands, unapologetically, to be seen, working to reduce shame and stigma around disability and facial difference, to challenge discrimination and challenge the narrow perception of what is considered 'normal'.

Carly has written a book, *Say Hello*; been painted for the Archibald Prize; edited Black Inc.'s *Growing Up Disabled in Australia*; and had a podcast, *Refreshments Provided*. She also has a Master of Communication and a heaving work and social life, and Bob Evans sang at her wedding.

I'm an only child, and until I was ten I went to school and grew up in Walla Walla, a tiny rural town of about five hundred people near Albury, NSW. My parents were migrants from England and South Africa who met and fell in love in Cape Town and moved to Australia to marry because of apartheid – Dad's white and Mum's black. Walla Walla was Lutheran, very religious, and the most religious of the people there saw mixture of race as a sin.

There were really only two things to do in Walla Walla: Sunday school or sport. Primary school was sporty, and you were grouped into scripture classes according to your religion. Mum went to church, so they put me in 'Anglican'. Mum and Dad sent me to Sunday school and then to youth group to make friends. There weren't any secular options. At Sunday school I was told that if I'd been born in Jesus's time, I'd have been a leper.

At youth group, which I'd attended wearing a very posh outfit, including one of those hats with a flower that the band Girlfriend wore, I was told my skin was red because I was paying for my parents' sins. A priest from one denomination told my parents I wouldn't get better unless they came to his church and were saved. It wasn't everyone, but the theories certain segments of Christianity had around being cursed and punished for it were just gross.

My skin is red because of ichthyosis. It's a rare and severe genetic skin condition. I was born with it and there are no cures, only treatments. It causes my skin to build up and scale and become extremely dry, and I apply paraffin-based ointment to my entire body twice a day to keep it moist. At birth I was prescribed sorbolene, which my parents used until I was in late primary school, so my face was always red, white and patchy.

I got golden staph when I was born (and throughout my life), because ichthyosis makes you susceptible to infections. I was in and out of hospital a lot through my childhood, and at primary school my bare legs were always getting infected because they made me wear a short skirt and wouldn't make allowances. I will always get infections. I shed skin, my skin is often sore, it itches – and ichthyosis also affects my eyes and ears, my digestive system and temperature regulation. I was a happy baby, but '24/7'. Mum and Dad decided not to have more children. They were new migrants without family support in a small rural town.

They were resourceful and just got on with it. Their attitude was, 'This is how it is – toughen up,' and a lot of my resilience comes from them. They showed me plenty of love and care: Dad read me stories, Mum would braid my hair. They did a wonderful job, and their mantra for me was, 'You're going to be normal. You're going to do everything that other people do. You're going to school, you're going to go to university and you're going to get a job.' This was very defined for me.

English people – and people of colour – can sometimes deny uncomfortable things and don't talk about them. That was my parents. I was told, 'You should just get on with it. It's not that bad; other people have it worse.' You know the attitude: 'Don't waste food, there are children starving in Africa.' When I was in hospital, they'd sometimes show me wards with children sicker than me, like, with burns or cancer, to give me perspective. And it did. But in hindsight, those kids weren't my 'teaching moment'. Who wants to be someone that a less sick kid comes to look at? I wouldn't want to be that.

At primary school I was called 'redskin' or 'skinner' or 'traffic light', names that stuck with me for all of my schooling. Apart from being spat on or pushed off my bike, there wasn't any physical bullying, so there are advantages when no one wants to touch you. Overt exclusion is worse than name-calling, I think.

Mum discovered flies buried in my ears when I was four. They'd been attracted by the smell of infected skin. It took an operation to remove them and for years I wore an insect net to school. I was so sad that only flies wanted to be near me. Other kids were grossed out by my skin and creams, and they'd freak out if I touched them. No one would sit next to me or sit where I'd been or hold my hand. Kids would braid each other's hair but no one would touch mine. I wasn't invited to birthday parties. 'Outcast' is a strong word but you definitely know when you are cast out by your peers. The loneliness is terrible.

I'd complain, but the teachers refused to believe me. 'Are you imagining it?' they'd ask. Or, 'What did you do to bring this on?' or, 'What can you do to change this?' or, 'Are you sure?' or, 'Are you overthinking?' Their lack of empathy was punitive. What could I possibly have changed? I think now that they'd never experienced prejudice and doubted its existence. I think they had comfortable lives in a very, very white small town. My mum was the only Black person in town. Kids would whisper, 'Your family's black!' Like I didn't know.

What else is there to do but complain? My parents instilled a strong sense of right and wrong in me. But if you talk about this stuff, *you're* seen as the troublemaker, a dibber dobber: 'Oh, she's being difficult again.' Australia has a difficult relationship with speaking up. There's an idea that speaking out is about making trouble rather than telling the truth. I understand this well because now I speak up all the time. My parents would confront the children and their parents, which didn't help at all. We were known as *that* family.

My self-worth was low. When I was nine, I wanted to kill myself, which is hard to say. I'd had enough of being different and excluded. I told Mum I didn't want to be here anymore and that I was going to get a knife. They rushed me to a child psychologist. I was okay after that but I don't remember that stage of life at all.

I spent a lot of time out of school getting treatment, sometimes for weeks at a time. There was school at the Royal Children's Hospital and I felt much more that I belonged there. The teachers 'got' me – they were there specifically to teach kids who were sick. The other students 'got' me – they were also sick. I made deep relationships and friendships there. I still have friends from hospital, although a number of them have died. That's the reality of living with disability or illness: people sometimes do have shorter lives.

I didn't identify as disabled at school. I didn't know I could. I didn't know I was. I'd never seen anyone like me. Media representation of disability was people on *A Current Affair* 'rorting the system', or the occasional Paralympian. There was one student with a severe disability, cerebral palsy, and she had a support worker, as she should have. The help she needed and received was obvious. I could do a lot more on my own than she could, and anyway I didn't feel I had the authority to ask for what I needed. I didn't feel disabled *enough*. I'm proud to identify as disabled now and advocate for access and inclusion, but all I wanted then was to be 'normal'. If I'd asked to wear trousers instead of a skirt, or to be excused from sport, I'd have worried about being further outcast.

I was very self-sufficient from an early age. Besides hospital, there'd be time off at home with infections. I was often indoors, left to my own devices, hand-sewing Barbie clothes, building doll houses and stuff like that. I really enjoyed being creative and amusing myself. The mobile library would come to town once a week and I read a lot – voraciously, beyond my years. Books kept me company and transported me away.

I was also really buoyed by music and fandom. My sense of fandom, my passion for music and musicians, is still huge. I still fangirl over Darren Hayes. I think a lot of disabled people have a strong sense of fandom. If you're excluded, you turn to things like books and music, where you're not going to be rejected. It's the attachment to someone so famous they're almost fictional, who you're never going to meet, and it's a way to connect to other people. I had a lot of penpals as a kid through *TV Hits* and *Smash Hits*, and the Savage Garden Fan Club.

There was a prestigious Lutheran high school in Walla Walla, and Mum and Dad wanted me to apply for a scholarship. I was a good student; I probably would have got in. I hated the exclusion of school, but I loved the learning. I just couldn't imagine another six years with those people. So I went to high school in Albury, which was better because it was secular, but I didn't find acceptance. Albury was different, though: by Year 12 there had been, like, eight teenage pregnancies.

There was so much loneliness. I spent a lot of my time in the library and a lot of time hanging around outside waiting for the library to open. Sometimes it was just shut for some reason, sometimes Mum dropped me off before 8.30am. There were some long waits with no one to talk to and nowhere else to go. But not being socially included made me an excellent student. I spent my lunchtimes in the library, and in Years 11 and 12, when I could finally opt out of sport, I had this little room upstairs to myself. I had my Discman and I'd listen to Silverchair and U2. I bought Paul Kelly's and Neil Finn's books of lyrics and read them over and over. I'd write poetry, read, do my own creative writing.

When the internet came in, like '96, '97, it changed how I connected with people. The librarian told me off for looking at Savage Garden on the library computer and said, 'Why don't you look up people with your experiences?' I did, and found people with ichthyosis. Not photos, of course – it was hard to put photos on the internet back then – but I connected with other people like me.

I've formed so many relationships online, met so many people in chatrooms: music fans and boys. I could choose when I wanted to tell people about my skin, when and whether I showed them my photo. I didn't have to endure that weird kind of meeting first-up. There was freedom online.

I wasn't entirely on my own. Around Years 8, 9 and 10, I was friends with other students who were all outcast. That helped. And in Year 9 I bonded over Savage Garden with a girl I'd known from primary school. Her family ran the pub and her parents had looked after me when mine were at work. We were really close and had a friendship based around Savage Garden for two or three years. We went to concerts, we waited outside Darren Hayes's hotel – it was incredible. I'd never had a friend before. It dissolved in the end and I think it was the pressure from other people, the embarrassment of being seen with someone different. I really missed her.

But ... I had no idea what a good friend was. All I knew was how I was treated, so if I *did* get a friend, I'd bitch about them or backstab them in some way. I was always retaliating or on the defensive. I wasn't a bad kid, but I didn't know how to be a friend because I didn't have any.

I didn't get enough socialisation. I could consume media, but didn't have friends or siblings to discuss them with. When I was eleven, Dad brought a joke book home from work for me to read, which I did. We went to a dinner party where there were other kids, and I told them a joke that had the c-word in it. I had no idea what it meant, didn't have friends to tell me. My parents whipped me out of there *so* fast, and we never went back.

In Year 12, Mum told me I had to get a part-time job. I put my résumé in at Kmart, expecting nothing, and ... I got a job. It saved me. Up until Kmart I'd been reactive and combative, just to get people to *stop*. To shut down the laughter. And customers *would* laugh, and say, 'You look sunburned', or ask what was wrong with me. I was once referred to as 'the lobster over there'. So my managers talked with me about how to deal with rude people.

These were big conversations at seventeen. 'Am I allowed to refuse service if someone is rude to me while I'm in uniform? Am I allowed to say, "Shut up," or "Mind your own business"?' At Kmart I could talk about my illness and appearance assertively. I could refuse to serve people. I didn't have to explain myself or answer to anyone. I learned professionalism. It changed my life.

I worked there for three and half years, and I made friends that I still have. I earned $23 a week, and it gave me my own life. I was able to come to Melbourne, and buy CDs and clothes. Kmart saved me and my parents made me stronger. Mum started sending me to Melbourne to stay with friends of hers when I was sixteen or seventeen, on the train on my own, no mobile phone. Like I said, self-sufficient. I always imagined living in the city: my plan was to get out, away from the bullying, and be a journalist.

My parents wanted me to have a secure and stable job for life, and I did, too. They couldn't afford to send me away, and my health was still unstable, so I had to attend university in Albury. They didn't offer journalism, so I did a very dull business degree, then did move to Melbourne and worked a very boring, stable government job where I couldn't be myself. I found my way into the media through blogging.

The media doesn't represent people like me positively, so I stopped hiding away, made myself visible and wrote myself in. I decided to stand out so that other people with skin and facial differences would feel less alone. I chose the path I wanted to go down. My career is shaped the way I want, and mostly I don't do things I don't want to do. Freelancing works better for me because it's flexible and I can manage my rest and treatments. A safe, secure job working five days straight is harder.

I'm at ease with being quirky now, and dressing in ways that draw attention rather than deflect it. I wear bright colours because they make me feel f**king fabulous. I used to be conservative. I didn't want to be looked at more than I already was. I had this amazing gold jacket that I would never wear because, 'Oh my god, it's too out there.' Now I just don't care. The louder the better, you know?

The more people tell me to stop being visible – and they do – the more visible I become. I don't take what people say on board and, the more ableist they are, the better the content they're giving me. I genuinely think it makes them look silly. I have the maturity to compartmentalise now. Being critiqued on what I've written is different to, 'You're so ugly, you need to kill yourself and die.'

It's all just navigating being on social media and having a profile. I have good boundaries. I block quickly, I've got autoresponder on my emails, I limit who can comment. I don't read the comments. Oh, sometimes I do – they're quite funny. I contact the authorities. I share what people send me, how they treat me, what messages I get sent. I'm not afraid to say, 'Hey, this person has hurt me, and others, a lot. Would you like more information?' I live my values. It can make me more of a target but it's important. I'm representing for a lot of people who *aren't* visible, who can't be.

I've got so much resilience and armour from being bullied at school and years of blogging and activism. I've got thick skin! Even though my physical skin is thin. I can take it. This stuff isn't for the faint-hearted, but it's easier to do difficult work when you're used to criticism.

The difference is that I choose how I put myself on show now, and that's a big difference. I had a few dates once with a man who was an academic in disability. I'd met him after I gave a high-profile speech at Federation Square. Things were progressing, then over dinner he told me he was uncomfortable with me being public, telling my story and doing disability activism. I didn't see him again.

I always overcompensated for how I looked, developing great skills to distract from what people might be thinking about my face. I can be funny and entertaining, make small talk, make people laugh, tell a good story. I'm very good at it. I'm no longer trying to distract, but it's useful being able to make conversation, talk to strangers or make people feel comfortable. I've done that right through my life, and so much of what I do is still putting people at ease.

As a public figure, I might be the only disabled person someone encounters, which is ridiculous, but I want them to have a good experience. It does always end up being on us to teach how language should be used around disability. I also feel a responsibility to put children at ease around difference, to be approachable. But I'm done with apologising for myself. I'm not impolite but I'm direct. I won't say, 'I'm sorry, if this offends you,' I'll say, 'This was hurtful and this is why.' I won't be silent. I have a whole list of access needs now, and they're not particularly glamorous, but I'm not going to apologise for needing a hotel room with a bath.

There's a societal expectation that you will be stoic. Every day there are barriers and discrimination. One time, working my government job and travelling into the city at peak hour, I asked for a seat. A man argued with me. 'Why do you need a seat? If you're disabled, you wouldn't be going to work.' That sort of stuff happens a lot: 'You're not disabled.' And then you have to go to work and get on with your day. There's no calling in with, 'I don't feel right. I've just been discriminated against, so I can't come in.'

Sometimes the work is lonely. I've had taxi drivers refuse to take me, saying I smell, that I'll ruin their taxi. And when I've written about it, people respond that I should go to Uber, or have a regular driver, or that my husband, Adam, should pick me up. And I do those things. But *sometimes* I just want to hail a cab. And, you know what? I should be able to. So should every disabled person. The taxi company ended up introducing a training video on discrimination. This is the work.

I grew up in fear of pissing people off. But now, given I've spent a lot of time not being liked, what's another 'not being liked' gonna do to me? What's another hater? I weigh up the cost to me of what I put out, and sometimes it's not worth it, but I care a lot less about who I'm not liked by. The important thing is that I've got good friends around me and a husband who loves me, and that my life is highly social. I know how to be a friend now.

I also realise that those kids who excluded me at school weren't actually people I'd want to be friends with. I went to the tenth anniversary of Year 12, and they'd mostly had children and stayed in the area. We had nothing in common. It was the *idea* of being part of a group that had enticed me. It was the *idea* of a friendship circle that I'd wanted.

There's freedom in not being popular. I really like Savage Garden, right, and they were a 'daggy' band. It was way cooler to like Pearl Jam. But I was used to people not liking me, so another level of dagginess made no difference. Savage Garden was just my thing. You reach a point where you go, 'Well, there's nothing to be done here; I might as well do what I want.'

There are only a few photos of me as a child. I didn't feel worthy of being seen and would screw my face up, trying to hide. I wish I could have seen myself through my eyes now. I was so cute! So worthy of smiling for a photo. There aren't photos from school. Kids didn't want to be photographed with me. I've had jobs where my work colleagues left me out of group photos. For a long time I worked to not be seen as someone who would embarrass people. That's changed completely now. I take *so* many selfies.

Sometimes, when I see teenagers on the train, it can snap me back to school. I still find sniggering hard to deal with. And there used to be parties where I didn't know people and I'd be on my own feeling awkward and thinking, 'Oh god, this feels like high school again.' But my work's changed everything because I've made myself visible. My profile has grown and people know me and my advocacy, and they're interested. Now they want to know me. I'm not saying that a large social media following equates to closeness – it doesn't. But the internet helps me find people and helps people find me.

I don't have quiet times at parties anymore, or in general, because people want to talk to me, be seen with me – and be photographed with me. I get so many opportunities and I'm constantly on the go. My life is fun. I don't have downtime, so I have to book alone time in for myself. It's so different to school and growing up that it's almost ... weird. I'm lucky, I think, that I had so much time to read, create and write. I wouldn't have this life if it weren't for my experiences. I wouldn't be so strong.

CHARLIE
PICKERING

Middle-class, white, intelligent, confident, from a stable home, on the hockey team, not ugly, and yet, somehow, Charlie Pickering still managed to be duffed up on a regular basis. A smart-arse from way back, his private school days are a grand reminder that just because you fit in and have privilege out the wazoo, it's no guarantee you won't be singled out.

Ultimately, being targeted has worked to Charlie's advantage; it gave him a strong social conscience, a willingness to speak truth to power, and the determination to pursue happiness. A trained lawyer, he turned his back on the law to pursue his true love, comedy. Melbourne-based Charlie did the hard yards in stand-up and emerged as one of Australia's most high profile television talents; he was the Generation X team captain on Channel Ten's *Talkin' 'Bout Your Generation* and a long-time co-host of Channel 10's *The Project*, before leaving to host his own prime time news satire show on the ABC, *The Weekly with Charlie Pickering*.

Besides being a politics, justice and breaking news obsessive, Charlie wrote *Impractical Jokes*, an affectionate book about his dad and best friend's escalating practical-joke war. Charlie remains unswervingly outspoken, committed to fairness and punching up, not down. Unusual in the world of stand-up comedy. He considers that being bullied has prepared him well for life in the public eye; hostile tweets from disenchanted viewers are water off a duck's back when you spent your high school years antagonising bullies stronger, and slower, than you, then ducking. Also, he knows how to sue for libel.

I went to an all-boys private school and it had a strong anti-bullying policy. They were very much on about it in assembly, saying often that bullying would not be tolerated and would be punished. They'd go into detail about how physical bullying is bad, but psychological bullying is worse, so you don't have to be beating someone up to be bullying them. Bullying was discussed and it was understood. But it didn't stop it from happening.

For me, bullying took a few forms. I was smaller than everyone else; I skipped a grade so I was almost a year younger. I was a late physical bloomer, I wasn't the kid that out of nowhere hit puberty like a freight train and all of a sudden had muscles and a beard. I was never that kid. I still can't put on muscle really. I wasn't big, and so I'd get physically intimidated by people, and I would be bullied by the guys who were always the big dumb jocks that went and did weights at lunchtime.

There was a definite hierarchy, with jocks at the top, nerds at the bottom, and everyone else in the middle. The most important thing was rowing. We were always made aware that the rowers were working very hard for the glory of the school. They train so much, they get up so early and they work so hard, so we all have to pull together and show some support for the rowers.

That in itself fed this culture that the biggest and strongest were at the top of the chain, and the smallest and weakest were at the bottom. The great irony of it was that every mid and end-of term, everyone got an academic ranking, with the top five for each year published in the school newsletter that went out on the Friday afternoon. There was this sudden highlighting of academic achievement in a very competitive way, so everyone had to care about their marks, and if you were the kind of person who studied a lot instead of lifting weights, it was your time to shine.

When I started there in Year 8 I didn't know what rankings were; my previous school hadn't done that. After a semester I came in at number 40 (out of 123), and I'm a very competitive person, so I was like, 'I'm sure I could do better than that.' I got my name in that newsletter relatively quickly, once I knew that there were rankings. Like I said, I'm competitive.

If you made the top five it was seen as an achievement, and the teachers would say 'well done', but generally in the playground and around the school it didn't mean you were on level-pegging with the captain of the football team, or the captain of boats, the stroke of the first eight rowing side. Yeah, yeah, I went to school in England in the 1800s.

I was very good at hockey. I was actually in the first hockey team for three years. But that's not a cool sport to be good at. You know, like, on the food chain of sports, that's well down the list.

The bullying happened in Years 9, 10 and 11. I'd get pushed around, physically intimidated, tripped over, shoved into walls. There was a guy in my basketball team, Sam, and he'd throw the ball at my head. From behind. We were on the same team, so you'd think you'd be okay, but he was very aggressive towards me. I'd get duffed up between classes because that's when we were unsupervised. It wasn't all the time, it would come and go. There'd be periods where I was targeted, and then they'd mess with me at every opportunity. It wasn't the physical aspect so much as never knowing when they were going to be there. I was always on edge.

Kind of the worst was when someone would be threatening me throughout the day with the idea of an impending beating after school, and so I'd go through the whole day thinking I was going to have the shit beaten out of me. I'd be thinking, how can I get from roll call, out of the school and home, so that I can escape this? That's just awful, the psychological side of it. I think the teachers were right; it is the worst. It's much worse than the physical side; a beating is never as bad as you think it's *going* to be.

I'd just get teased and picked on. I had a smart sense of humour and was quick with the comebacks, but that would escalate what was going on. It was a blessing and a curse – I had a weapon and a defence mechanism, but it often got me in trouble. The problem with having a comeback is you have the ability to make the bully look small in front of his friends, because they've inevitably said something really dumb to give you shit. And that's when they escalate to violence. I've had guys say, 'Right, you're f**ked,' jump over a table and throw me to the ground because I said something that cut them down to size.

The advantage, I guess, to the anti-bullying policy, was that when I would get bullied I knew it was wrong. At no point did I think I was bringing it on myself. But it doesn't mean you can do anything about it. I mean, the last thing you're going to go and do is dob a bully in to the headmaster. You feel that's only going to make it worse.

The idea of physical supremacy in a school hierarchy is celebrated everywhere. It's how it is. I was sort of in the middle. I wasn't one of the nerds, hiding in the library at lunchtime, but I wasn't one of the bigger, tougher athletes or in the cool group either. The middle was a good place to be, I thought. My group of friends all found the same stuff funny, and the most important thing was our sense of humour. I was lucky to have that group around so I never felt entirely alone. That said, when the bullying happened I'd feel instantly alone. It doesn't matter who you're friends with because it's one person picking on you directly and you feel threatened and intimidated, and it's an instantly solitary experience.

There wasn't an undercurrent of racism, as far as I know. The Asian students hung out together in what was called 'Chinatown' but no one was pulling their eyes at the side and putting on bad Mickey Rooney accents. There was actually a sense of curiosity; they had cool gadgets and were the first to get mobile phones. We thought they were from the future. I don't recall economic prejudice either. We lived in a very affluent suburb, and it was an affluent school. The scholarship kid was good at footy, so you weren't going to pick on him. There were academic scholarships, but they'd be picked on for being geeks over being on a scholarship. But kids did get bullied, and it shows that even in a wealthy private school, where you take away real financial disparity between kids, people will still find a reason to pick on someone. It's like water finding the lowest point.

I don't *really* know why people picked on me. Maybe I bit back just enough to draw attention. I never hesitated putting my hand up in class. I didn't hold back or try to make a small target out of myself, and I was a class clown and a bit of a smart-arse. But I didn't throw up any major red flags on a bullying profile. I wasn't any of the usual laundry list of arsehole reasons to pick on somebody for something completely beyond their control. I wasn't poor, fat, gay, black, stinky, asthmatic, particularly uncoordinated or disabled. Maybe that was part of the point: there wasn't a particular reason.

There's always going to be bullying, I think. It's part of nature – big strong shit eats the small weak shit. But as much as it seems when you're in high school that the big, good-looking, stronger, faster kids are going to rule the world forever, it levels out in time.

It could be very hard, and sometimes I had to lie to everyone to give off the air that I didn't care. It took some acting sometimes. But I reckon the best way to disempower a bully is to not care about the bullying. It takes away their reason for doing it, if they're just like a fly buzzing around an elephant.

I never let it damage my self-esteem. There were days when I felt shitty, or threatened, or intimidated, and I would wish I was bigger and stronger and could do something about it, but at no point did I take it on board and think, 'Maybe I deserve this? Maybe I am this shit.'

I've never gone to a psychologist to talk about when I was bullied; I don't feel I need to. I'm happy, but maybe there is something that has seeped in. The idea that you should always try to make the right thing happen. Not right for you, just the right thing. I guess that's an overarching goal.

Being bullied definitely affected my political outlook. It's really given me a sense that governments shouldn't be there to serve the strongest and richest; governments should be there to serve the weakest and poorest. I don't like bullies in any form and I will always, always take the side of the victim in a bullying situation. That's the flipside of bullying – you should always stick up for those who have no one to stick up for them.

I'm not intimidated by anyone, either. It doesn't matter who I meet. Okay, sometimes I might get giddy because, I mean, like I met Lou Reed and I was a little bit, 'Holy shit, I'm in the same room as Lou Reed,' but I wasn't intimidated. That's good and bad; early on in my current career it may have been interpreted as arrogance. It wasn't even confidence. It was just, 'I won't let myself be intimidated.'

I think, actually, that being bullied made me more resourceful; I have the idea that if things are hard I know I can dig a little bit deeper to get through something. Nothing is so bad that I'm not going to get through it. I've got a pattern of learned behaviour, which is, 'Something shit happened to me and I got through it, and things are okay.'

I was well into history, and that helped. I would often go, 'People survived proper hard stuff, why should I get to feel bad?' Being picked on by the big kid is nowhere near as bad as war, or death camps, or starving on the streets of India or Africa. Learning about real suffering made it really clear that my bad day was nowhere near as bad as the best day of someone else. Heaps of people have a much worse day than you.

It also made me determined to not be unhappy. I studied law, but I'm not a lawyer, because it was *never* going to make me happy. I love the law, I'm fascinated by it, but I started work in a law firm and in my first week I looked at the guys in the corner offices. The senior partners – who, in the realm of the law were considered very successful – were 40 kilograms overweight, didn't really know their wives, barely remembered the names of their kids and couldn't remember the last time they had a holiday.

I want to succeed in whatever I do, but I just looked at them and thought, 'If this is success then it's not for me.' So I burned that bridge, rolled that dice, and I went back to what I wanted to do since I was ten, and that was to be a comedian. It didn't pay off straight away; it took a really long time. And all my lawyer friends have made a lot more money than I have. But it's taken its toll; they're all bald and look way older.

To me it boils down to 'Why not?' Like, why *not* be one of the people who wins? Like, if you've got a choice, if your choice is between winning and losing, why not try for winning? You can do nothing and lose. Anyone can lose. Why not have a crack at winning, what's the worst that can happen? If you lose then, at least you know you didn't lose because you didn't try. In my mind I think undeserving people win all the time. So why not try? It's amazing what you can do when you tell yourself that you can do it.

In terms of my work, the advantage to having been bullied is I don't let the haters get to me. I get cyber-bullied – there are things written on websites about me that are horrific – but I'm old enough to know that it is utterly meaningless. If it crossed into the real world and someone came after me physically, that's different. But in a grown-up realm there are laws against that shit.

What people say about me doesn't bother me, it never will. I mean, this happens: people will say on Twitter that they want me killed. They genuinely say that they would like me to be killed. But if you listen to everyone who has something nasty to say about you, you'd never get anything done, you'd be a wreck. I'm not letting that damage my self-confidence. Who cares? Who cares what people say?

In the end it's all meaningless. Who gives a f**k what a bully thinks? Who gives a shit what some idiot at school thinks? You're going to agree and disagree with thousands of people in your lifetime, so why let one get through to you?

When I look back at the kids that bullied me, I reckon they had shitty parents. My guess is they had a pretty crap time at home, and they were taking it out on someone else. But I have no sympathy for them. I'm sorry they had a shitty house to go home to, but that's not my fault, lots of people have problems, and they don't take it out on someone who doesn't deserve it.

The thing is, high school is formative, but it's a tiny part of your life, and every year that goes by you realise it more and more. None of it is there forever, and it becomes a very small part of your life. By the time you're 22 you think the sixteen-year-old you was a bit of a dick. By the time you're 25 you think the 22-year-old you was a bit of a dick. By the time you're 30, if you look at the sixteen-year-old you, you'll say, 'What *were* you thinking?'

ALICE
PUNG

Alice Pung is one of Australia's quiet achievers. Modest and grounded, Alice determinedly does things her way. She's a beloved writer and educator known for her two acclaimed memoirs *Unpolished Gem* and *Her Father's Daughter*, two novels *Laurinda* and *One Hundred Days*, and collection of essays, *Close To Home*. *Unpolished Gem*, a comedic portrait of family life in multicultural Footscray, won the Australian Book Industry Award's Newcomer of the Year Award and established her career.

Alice's school years were dominated by her home duties; as the eldest in a migrant family, she was responsible for her younger brother and two sisters while her parents worked. She began writing a diary when she was eight, venting her many frustrations about screaming siblings, and mothers who insisted on selfishly having more babies.

A refugee who was 'smuggled' into Australia by her eight-month pregnant mother, Alice is the product of that collision between her parents culture, and white Australia's. She writes eloquently on race, class, and the tensions between parents and children in migrant families.

Besides contributing regularly to *The Monthly*, *Good Weekend* and *The Australian*, Alice is also a minimum-wage lawyer, artist-in-residence at Melbourne University's Janet Clarke Hall, and a pastoral care worker. Growing up understanding that hard work and a good education was her ticket out of the 'burbs, and suffering a stress-related breakdown in Year 11, Alice is committed to supporting the next generation of schoolchildren.

The biggest stress for me wasn't school, it was being the eldest of four children. I spent my childhood and adolescence looking after my younger siblings at home. Before my dad got into the Retravision franchise, he had this little watch shop, and he worked very long hours trying to get his businesses running. My mother was an outworker; she worked 14-hour days in the garage.

It wasn't like *The Baby-Sitters Club*. You couldn't hand the baby back. I had to clothe them, prepare the formula milk, the nappies, everything, and my youngest sibling is twelve years younger than me. That was a big stress, being responsible for these little lives. So I wasn't stressing about schoolwork. The schoolwork was fine. I liked schoolwork. I was stressing about whether my sister would put her hand on an iron or something.

School was the place you were able to study. Me and my friends would always be in the library, because they had similar circumstances. My friend Roslyn's dad, for example, drove a taxi, so she was looking after younger ones as well. The librarians loved us, and even though Roslyn wasn't Asian they'd say, 'Oh, these Asian kids are really good. They're very hard working.'

The library was a way out. I could say to my parents, 'I'm going to the library,' and my mum would say, 'Fine, just take your sister with you.' I couldn't say, 'Hey, I'm going to the movies,' or 'I'm going bowling,' because my mum was working in the garage. I'd feel too guilty.

There was never time to worry about fitting in, or clothes, or the cool group. At every school I went to, there would be a group of migrants, and they'd be the girls I'd relate to and hang with. And migrants didn't give a toss about social status, or have slumber parties, or shop for dresses, or hang out at Highpoint to look for the St John's boys. We all saw school as a place to learn, and knew we had to work really hard and get good grades.

Fortunately, we didn't stand out. My friends who weren't, like me, looking after their families, sewed for their parents who were outworkers. That meant, actually, we were quite well dressed. One of my friends' parents sewed clothes for Sportsgirl and Country Road, and once in a while they'd go to Vietnam and get us fake designer bags.

There were certainly no boys around. With migrant girls, you're meant to be virginal until marriage. So the concept of a boyfriend when you're fifteen or sixteen is pretty abstract. What would you do with a boyfriend? Study with them? A boyfriend might be something you're wistful about at night but it's not something you obsess over. There's no time for that.

My parents weren't 'tiger' parents though. There was never any overt pressure, or being told I had to become a lawyer or doctor, mostly because my mother couldn't read or write so there was no way she was going to force anything on me. She was eight months pregnant with me when they arrived in Australia. She was one of those 'queue jumpers'; she lied about how advanced her pregnancy was, because she knew they wouldn't let her on the plane otherwise. She was very skinny, and says that's how she smuggled me in.

My difficulty was in not knowing what I wanted to be, only what I didn't. My big dream was to get out of Footscray, to be honest. There's all this expectation if you grow up in a small community. Every small business owner knows everyone else. My dad always had this dream, he said, 'Well, if you become a doctor or lawyer or accountant or a dentist, we'll build another storey above our shop and you can practise there.' That was common and I really didn't want to be stuck in Footscray above my dad's shop. It's wonderful to be connected to a community but sometimes it's a curse.

It wasn't the people; I mean, my family and friends are in Footscray. It was the doing the same things every day and the mentality of scarcity. Middle-aged housewives who've been through war, been through genocide in Cambodia, almost having a heart attack over strawberries that are priced twenty cents more than they should be. There was an expectation that you put your roots down and live a very safe life, and you shouldn't go far because then you're not watched over. I found it stifling, and frightening, and insular.

My brother and I went to the same primary school for seven years, in Braybrook, an industrial heartland near Footscray. We were a refugee family and part of a small handful of Asian kids. Race-wise it wasn't really a problem, and I had friends at the school, but it was the late 1980s, there was a recession on and a lot of people on the dole, and these beat-up old Holdens would follow us and tell us to, 'Go home and stop stealing our jobs.' But I was eight, I didn't understand.

By the 1990s a lot of my friends' parents were starting to support One Nation. When I was thirteen or fourteen I'd go to their houses and see big posters of Pauline Hanson stuck on the wall. It made me anxious because I knew what that symbolised. But they always treated me and my brother kindly, and I realised people's politics didn't necessarily reflect who they were. Some older people would say, you know, 'Maybe we shouldn't allow too many chinks in, but your family is okay.'

I changed high schools five times. My father believes you should always better yourself, and he kept changing up the schools I went to. I liked the moving from school to school, to be honest, because you could start anew. I think it would be harder to stay in one school, because you get stuck, and the sort of person you are gets cemented.

Like at home, me and my brother were noisy and told jokes, but at primary school we were 'the quiet Asian kids who were good at art.' At least it was positive. We lived in a bogan neighbourhood – we were Asian bogans! – we could easily have been labelled 'the chinks'. So I took on different identities at the different high schools, and each year I'd keep the friends that really meant something and leave the politics and little group formations behind.

First up I went to a girls school in Footscray, and there was a huge refugee influx. I'd be in classrooms with kids who were a lot older than us, fifteen- and sixteen-year-olds in Year 7. They'd just never been educated in the camps. I had a nice group of newly arrived Vietnamese friends. Some of them didn't speak much English, but because they were so much older they treated me like I was their younger sister, and I enjoyed that. These were strong girls, and one of my best friends to this day spent her first twelve years in one room with seven siblings in a camp in Hong Kong.

It was a very mixed school, kids from camps in Thailand, Serbia and Bosnia, and very rough. Some girls would do things like leave condoms on your seat and pretend they were used. Every ten days or so there'd be a fight, a bunch of hair-pulling and things like that. This was before mobile phones, and there was a Year 8 informer who'd run around the school yelling about it, and we'd all go and watch.

In Asian culture there is a great respect for education and I was shocked that they'd pick on teachers. One day they stuck a tampon that had been soaked in water and red paint on top of the doorframe, and when the teacher walked in it fell and hit her in the face. The next year I went to a Catholic college, and the biggest deal was when someone's pencil case got stolen, and it was in the school newsletters for two weeks. 'Has anyone seen Mai-Lin's pencil case?' Seriously.

Dad had thought I'd be better off there, so he wrote a letter every couple of weeks to the Catholic school, reasoning with them, trying to talk them into taking me. Saying, if they took me, they could try and convert me. Some Asian parents just baptise their children to get them into the Catholic system but he didn't want to do that. I didn't know about it until my interview with the principal, when she pulled out the pile of letters, written on an old typewriter, and showed me. She said, 'We have to have you. These letters are great.' I was very touched that he did that for me.

It was lovely there and I felt confident. I got into all sorts of things, like debating and choir. Then Dad heard about a more academically focused private school in Essendon, and I went there in Year 10 even though he had to pay fees. After a year there he asked me if I'd like to redo the entry exam for a state-funded scholarship school, and I got in there for Year 11.

Getting into this school was a bit of a thing. Most of the Asian kids I knew were encouraged to take the exam in Year 8, and if you get in, it's like going to a private school from Year 9. I'd applied in Year 8 but didn't get in. My parents had very much wanted me to go, and paid a family friend to tutor me for weeks – and weeks and weeks – in maths, because that was my weak point. But, no, I was *really* bad at maths. In Year 11 they expanded the criteria and I got in through art.

So there I was, at this tough, competitive school. And, the thing is, you might have been the big fish in your school, but all of a sudden it's the cream of the crop from every other school. The brightest, most ambitious, competitive and, in some cases, ruthless, students in the one place. There *were* a bunch of new girls who came along with me, but we were all a bit anxious; we came in Year 11, we weren't the smart ones that got in in Year 9.

It didn't pan out too well. I got very depressed halfway through the year, had a kind of breakdown, and had to leave. I hadn't done the 'Asian Five' subjects – you know, the five subjects that Asian students do? It's two sciences or maths, English and a language, and it's carefully calculated to maximise your results in Year 12. Dad had been wonderful about that, *not* making me do them. He'd said, 'Look, if you're good at legal studies and literature, do that. Because you'll do well.'

But at that school, the entire focus was getting an ENTER score above 95 or 96. Anything below was almost a suicide mission. For most of the girls, this was their one chance to escape the crappy jobs their parents were doing, the working-class suburbs, and make something of themselves. *Such* pressure. And I had no maths or science subjects up my sleeve. Absolutely none. I constantly felt anxious and not very bright.

All schools want to stay high in the school ratings. But this place was ruthless, and I didn't know how to play whatever game it was. Girls would hide books in the library, so they could go back to them and no one else could find them. The girl who was the smartest at maths gave the wrong answers to anyone who asked her for help. Stuff like that: it was a bizarre atmosphere.

I don't know exactly what happened but after a while all I could think was, 'I can't stay in this school.' I struggled through term three. Just dragged myself along. I was so depressed. I had no energy. I was always sleepy. I'd go to my dad's store and nap upstairs near the boxes. I kept saying to myself, 'Only one term to go! I can do it!' But during the holidays I broke down, and I couldn't go back.

A contributing factor, I think, was that I didn't have a concrete plan. I knew I wanted to get out of Footscray, but besides the family doctor or our teachers, I had no idea what a 'professional' was. It was all abstract, stuff I'd got off television. Migrant communities – Greeks, Italians, Vietnamese, Chinese – are very business and status oriented. You get your business and then you build your big house in Caroline Springs, and I was never any good at business. It wasn't in me. A lot of my friends knew at sixteen what kind of house they wanted, and which career would get them that, and I've never been that sort of ambitious and I envied them for their decisiveness.

You know, at the other schools I went to, they noticed if you were sad or on the brink of going into depression. There was pastoral care, or the teachers knew what was going on in your life and helped you. They cared. This school? I fell between the gaps for months and no one noticed. If someone had only said, 'Oh, you're going through a tough time. Maybe we can work out how to help you.' But no one did.

Because, you know, my marks were still pretty good. I was just having a nervous breakdown.

After I broke down, Dad and I went to see the year level coordinator, and she was furious with me. There was no, 'What's happened to you these past few months? How are you? Why do you suddenly have to leave?' She just said, 'Fine. Go. Pack your stuff.' So I took my stuff and left. It was the most terrible way to leave.

I went back to my previous school for Year 12, and I was welcomed. The teachers were great; it was so different. They gave me half the year's work to see if I could catch up and because I'm good with humanities I did. It was such a huge relief, to realise I wasn't stupid.

That scholarship school gave me an important lesson. Asian culture is very hierarchical. You're taught from when you're really small to respect your elders because they've lived longer and they know more. And teachers are really respected by Asian kids; they know more than you and they pass that knowledge to you. You *never* think that you're smarter than a teacher. Friends who teach say you rarely get Asian or Indian parents coming in to say, 'Why did you give Johnny a bad mark?' They always say, 'How can Johnny do better?'

But that aspect, in some ways, was a bad thing to have that year. There are some people you can't respect because they're not decent people. They're bullies in their position of power. At the time there was no way I could have conceived of that, seen that a teacher could bully a student through apathy or neglect or deliberate exclusion.

In terms of my personality, I think going to a new school every year was a positive. It meant I couldn't be too contrarian – I couldn't assert my personality. You know, some people walk into a room and you know they've got a massive personality? That was never my thing.

If you have a big personality, people quickly determine where you slot in. I adapted. I'd spent a few months being quiet, and watching and waiting, and then I'd find my group of friends.

Fitting in is a useful skill: it's always helped me at work. I've always been able to get work easily, and I've never had to promote myself. Colleagues like working with me. A couple of times, when they've moved to another department, they've said, 'There's a vacancy, do you want to work up a level?' I'm good at fitting in to new institutions.

It's also very Asian to keep your head low and work hard, and it doesn't necessarily work outside of the public service. In the private sector, a lot of my female Asian friends, sadly, have got stuck in the same job, and not been promoted. They say, if you're hardworking, they'll just give you more work!

As a writer, going to a lot of different schools meant I was always an outsider, and I developed the outsider's eye that a writer needs to have. For perspective, and to make points of comparison. I'd go to a new school and think, wow, this is really different from the last one. Every school has a vibe, a method, a set of values that you wouldn't notice or understand unless you come from elsewhere. I learned that circumstances really affect people because every school had a group of people who were institutionalised – only acting a certain way because they were in that context. There's no such thing as an inherent sense of self or belonging, you behave differently depending on where you are. As a writer, that's invaluable.

And, no, my friends and I had no time to bother with clothes and boys, but that meant we had to focus. That discipline was really important. It sounds very uninspired but that's how it works. I force myself to write when I don't feel like it. If I didn't, I'd only write twice a year! But that's like everything, isn't it? To get through school you've got to force yourself to do a lot of work that's tricky to understand.

I started writing when I was eight, as a reaction to my situation at home. Not because I was a genius or anything, but because I was so frustrated. I was eight years old and looking after babies and, you know, they cry all the time. So there were two ways out: I could hurt one of my sisters, or I could write about it to divert that energy. As a boy you can go punch something or run around the backyard, but if I ran around my grandmother would say, 'Why are you running around, acting like a boy? Girls don't do this.' Writing was a very civilised way to get it out – it was purely an outlet.

I read back over my diaries and I think, what terrible things to write about your family. I never wrote that I wanted to hurt them, but I was so angry. 'F**k this family! F**k my mum!' 'Why did they have so many babies without consulting me?' That's the way you think as a nine-year-old.

I still keep a diary. It helps a lot. When I needed to speak, the emotional side of things was all there. I try to write every day, and if I'm not, I'm writing letters. Because I went to so many schools, I've got a lot of friends with very different lives.

Writing was never a professional option. I did a writing subject at university, and my tutor said the stories were good, and that I should submit them. I sent them to strange places, like *Woman's Day* and *New Idea*, because that was what I was reading. My idea of the pinnacle would have been to be published in *Reader's Digest*. She suggested literary journals I'd never heard of, *Meanjin* and *Southerly*, and eventually I was published. I thought, 'This is cool. I can do this, not for a living, but for fun.'

I could never write full-time. I need to have a self-sufficient source of income, otherwise I'd panic. I've inherited that need for security. I've always had a job, actually always had three going on at a time. I'm in the public service because it gives me a nice work–life balance. I wouldn't get that if I owned my own business in Footscray.

I wouldn't change anything for myself, and my experiences have made me a good pastoral worker. Students are able to talk to me because I don't assert my beliefs or tell them what to do. They usually know what to do themselves, anyway; they just need to talk about it.

I'm really aware of what kids need. It's so easy for the Asian kids, for immigrants, to fall through the gaps. Teachers leave you alone; they think you're okay because you're working hard in the library. They just don't understand there's all this stuff going on at home: kids to be looked after; the dad doing taxi shifts; midnight sewing sessions because an order needs to go out the next day. A friend of mine would come to school, all bleary eyed, and the teachers would say, 'Don't study so hard.' They had no idea.

Because of my experience, I'm committed to my job. I know what's happening with my students. If they've been in their room longer than three days, you know that they're down and out, or they're sick. They're not coddled but they're well looked after. No one will fall through the gaps here.

I particularly understand what's going on with the international students. I remember one student, who was nearly finished with a four-year accounting degree, but what she really wanted to do was this very technical mathematics philosophy course. The student counsellor had told her to change course and follow her passion. I said, 'So why did you come to me?' And she said, 'Oh, my parents sold the house in

China to send me here.' And I got it.

She couldn't change course. The aim was for her to get her parents to Australia through her education and her work. She just needed to hear that. I said, 'Look, after they come here, you'll be fine to do your philosophy course.' We calculated how many more years it would be and how much work she needed to do. It's unrealistic to follow your dreams sometimes, isn't it? Sometimes it's okay to accept things.

HOLDEN
SHEPPARD

For the longest time, Holden Sheppard, the Geraldton-born-and-raised YA author with an attitude, a mohawk and a Collingwood AFL membership, thought he was the only gay bogan. Living in a small regional WA city and being the youngest boy in a controlling, blue-collar Italian Catholic family, the realisation he was same-sex attracted came with a shit sandwich of despair, depression, drinking, denial, religious conversion therapy and a close call with thinking that dying was a solution.

Coming out was a catalyst for Holden's transformation into a bold, bolshy gym junkie, Pokémon-enthusiast punk who now lives a consciously visible life. But he'd been hiding since childhood, anxiously suppressing his personality to please his family, stay loved, avoid criticism and blend in. A high-achieving, bland, tightly wound kid, he was bullied at home and school, and escaped into reading books, books and more books. He began writing at seven, finally finding somewhere safe to be himself.

His gritty debut YA novel, *Invisible Boys*, won multiple accolades. Dark and raw, it explores sexual discovery when you're homosexual, working class and not safe in a small, intolerant Australian town. Since it was published, Holden's been contacted by countless 'invisible boys', innumerable utterly alone 'gay bogans' – Aussie blokes who can't come out because homosexuality isn't visible in their worlds, and so neither are they. His second novel, *The Brink*, is a deep dive into similar territory, and *Invisible Boys*, named a Notable Book by the Children's Book Council of Australia, is in development for television.

I read once that if you read a lot as a kid and then you stop when you're an adult, it's not that you don't like reading – you just found another, better way to dissociate. And, oh man, that made so much sense. I was an *avid* reader. I devoured books up until I was sixteen, when, like every teenager in Geraldton, I discovered alcohol. I reckon I dissociated until I was twenty. I really wasn't present for most of my childhood.

I was a repressed child, and I'm not even talking sexuality-wise – that wasn't until my teens. I was deeply anxious as a kid and obsessed with blending in and being well behaved. When I was five, in Year 1 at St Lawrence's Catholic primary school, my green crayon broke. I held in the panic, but when I got home, I was distraught. My parents were like, 'What the hell is wrong with you?' And I was horrified to tell them, because only bad kids let things like that happen, so it meant I was a bad kid. I was *that* tightly wound.

I wasn't popular, I think. Well, I *know*. I was on a low social rung at primary school. I wouldn't take part in things because I didn't want to get in trouble. I was the smart kid, the 'square'. The other kids were like, 'Just do the thing. Everyone else is,' and I was like, 'No, we must follow the rules and do the right thing.' I was clever and nerdy; that's all I had. I did well in tests, I could write, I was good at reading. I was well behaved.

I briefly hung with a few kids in the alternative crowd in Year 6 and Year 7, but I was on the outer. The first time we arranged to meet, to go to a Pokémon movie, I rocked up all excited and no one was there. No one had mobiles then, so it was like, 'Oh. Okay.' It was awful. The next day I asked what had happened, and they laughed: 'We deliberately told you the wrong cinema. We thought it'd be funny, hahaha.'

I was still low-rung at high school, but not absolute bottom in the 'reject' group. I was in a miscellaneous group of quiet, geeky guys who weren't footy players, surfers or stoner skaters. In Years 11 and 12, we multiplied our popularity a little by forming a bigger group of boys and girls, and some of them dated each other. The closest I got to a personality trait was quoting movies and TV shows. I was the 'king of quotes'.

My perception is that I wasn't liked, but I probably wasn't likeable. I didn't show up much *to* be liked. I kept myself busy, filled my lunch breaks and after school with stuff: the yearbook committee, the committee for the school's annual creative book of student work, the debating club, the school production. After school, I'd work at the supermarket three or four nights a week. Outside of that, homework! The busier you are, the less you can be seen.

I was just reproducing more good behaviour: 'I'm in this room. I'm doing extracurricular stuff like good kids do. There's a teacher present. This will go on my résumé one day.' I suppose I had some good times. I don't recall much of school. I'll get asked, 'Do you remember such and such from Year 10? Or this thing that went down?' And I am like, 'No.' Sure, I was there, but I wasn't *there*. I'd rock up to school, physically. Then I'd go home, physically. All fake. All a facade. Later, after I got away and processed, I realised I'd spent nearly twenty years being someone else. And not an interesting someone else, either. I was *beige*. I let nothing show.

I didn't have anything on my bedroom walls. There was wallpaper, stuff Mum put there. A crucifix. Awards from my Catholic high school. Framed family photos looking down and watching. I had zero presence and put zero personality on display. A kid should feel safe to express themselves in their own room, but it always felt safer to do nothing.

I went back when I was twenty, pulled it all down and put up footy posters, shit like that. Later I realised I was finally marking my territory, pissing around the edges of the room to claim it.

Growing up, I felt inferior. I was this tiny kid in a loud, noisy house full of teenagers. I'm number five of six kids – three boys, three girls – and there was a big age gap between my four older siblings and me. When I was five, my brothers were twelve and seventeen, big teenage boys. We're Italian, and in the house there were the eight of us, the dog and the cat, people visiting, friends coming over and cousins everywhere because Dad's one of eleven. At any given moment, a *lot* of people. I grew up surrounded by noise, feeling not big enough and inadequate. The family told me I was 'unco', so I was hugely socially anxious about sport and didn't play. I couldn't understand why I wasn't like my brothers. I was small, weak, sensitive. Not a normal boy. There had to be something wrong with me.

To people on the outside, I think our family life appeared happy and serene, but beneath the surface, it was as tempestuous and dysfunctional as any family – more so, in some ways. I grew up feeling alone, like I didn't fit in. I was extremely unhappy most of the time. I was so scared of losing people's love and approval. I felt, from a young age, that certain people's affection and approval was conditional upon good behaviour, obedience, conformity. To a small child, it was terrifying. I didn't want to have anyone stop loving me. That could never happen. It seemed clear that I must never do anything wrong and always had to be good. I became a very, *very* good kid, and highly stressed all the time.

I didn't feel that there was a safe way to say, 'I disagree,' or, 'That really hurt me.' If I said something bothered me, or had hurt me, someone else would say, 'No, it didn't. That didn't happen.' And I'm like, 'Right. Okay. Right. I guess it didn't.' My own feelings and perceptions of the world were not my own – they were up for scrutiny and reinterpretation – anything I said was broken down and challenged until I agreed. So, when bad things happened, I'd convince myself it didn't happen. It legit f**ked me up. I felt that self-expression was not just bad, but dangerous. I felt like I could not be myself, ever – not at school, not at home, not anywhere.

So I dissociated. Mostly I would read. And read and read. I loved maps, reading them and drawing them. When I was five years old, my parents bought me the 1994 Perth UBD street directory and I was genuinely stoked. When I was ten, my dream job of town planner was advertised in *the Geraldton Guardian*. I applied: 'Here you go, here are some of the maps I've drawn – these suburbs, these subdivisions.' I don't know what I was thinking. They replied offering me work experience when I was older. I didn't take it up, and I kind of wish I had. That was kind.

I read Enid Blyton: *The Magic Faraway Tree* and the Malory

Towers and St. Clare's series. I loved those boarding-school stories. But they were about British girls in the 1930s and I longed to see something set in the 1990s, with an Aussie boy in it. I wanted to see myself in there instead. So my writing career started with Enid Blyton knock-offs when I was seven. The main character was Jake, who was twelve – a big-boy age – and he went to boarding school.

From then on, that's what I did. On weekends and school holidays, I'd sit at the dining-room table and write. At first, I was excited, like, 'Look, I'm writing a book!' But Mum started to take it over, wanted to make it a publishing company for kids or something, and I was appalled. Writing was this tiny safe space I'd found for myself, and the only place I had where I could show up, say what I thought, and there would be no adult to control or humiliate me; where I could be Jake, a normal boy. I never mentioned my writing to family again. Ever. It became secretive. No one could see it. Friends once tried to wrestle the notebook from me, and I physically tore it in half. *No one* read my stuff.

Writing was where I lived my real life. And later, during high school, I went online. I was writing Pokémon fan fiction and found a forum with others, and we socialised after school. I'd log on under a different name and was free! I could be myself: sarcastic, funny and rude. I could argue and be angry. They were writers, like me: sensitive, willing to talk about weird stuff, have intellectual discussions and a laugh.

The writing community has always felt welcoming and permissive. Writers have empathy. They kind of see you, and treat you gently. English class was a haven too. I'm that kid who still goes back. Every three years or so, I make an appointment, go back to high school, bring my husband and visit my English teacher. I was lonely my whole life, and she was lovely to me.

Around age sixteen, my sexuality sent my mental health over the edge. Until then, well, denying your sexuality isn't hard when you're suppressing everything else. I had no inkling until I was nine and had a fleeting *something* looking at muscular bad guys on an X-Men cartoon. At twelve, I had a crush on Prince Caspian from the Narnia stories. At fourteen, the switch flipped, and it stopped being, 'I'm watching the footy with my family,' and became, 'Holy f**k, these guys are hot.' I had dreams about Collingwood players.

That *should* have been my sexual awakening. But I was practised at denying bad things were happening. An old puberty book, *What's Happening To Me?*, was lying around the house, and it said not to worry if you were same-sex attracted at fourteen, that it was a phase due to an early hormone surge. It was in a book, so it must be true. I'd be attracted to guys and go, 'That's not real. It's a *phase*.'

But by sixteen, I was post-pubescent, and still very attracted to men. *Shit.* This wasn't a phase, it was a big problem. Our family background is Sicilian-Australian, so being gay is super shameful. The word used is *finocchio*, or fennel; it's an Italian slur that translates to 'faggot'. It's beyond the pale. You'd get torn apart. And Dad's in earthmoving, my uncles are brickies. Blue-collar guys. Gay's not a thing. And we're Catholic. The message everywhere was, 'This is evil, it's a sin and it makes us sick to our stomachs.' I had the layer on top of it being impossible to be the bad kid. There was no way I could admit it. Never. I simply *couldn't* be gay.

I went into extreme depression. I *loathed* myself. I berated and punished myself for looking at guys, or for masturbating. I wanted to die. I started binge-drinking.

The only fix I could find was religious conversion therapy, and for three years I tried to 'pray the gay away', from sixteen to nineteen. It nearly did me in. I wasn't sent away to conversion therapy camp or anything, but I turned heavily to religion: praying to God, writing letters to God, poring over the Bible, reading American fundamentalist websites, and so on. They claim you can 'get rid of it'. It's pseudoscientific bullshit, and it was really traumatising. I became hyper-religious. I read the Bible, wore my crucifix and used it to pray every day. I wrote some really strange, awful shit to God. Letters about Satan, asking Jesus to save me. I became outspokenly anti-gay if the subject came up. I was an angry little homophobic goody-two-shoes.

It was a desperate time. I'd started webcamming and chatting to dozens of much older men – sexual experimentation with guys who, in hindsight, were predators. And I'd kind of get off, and immediately it was like, 'I've sinned again. Jesus is going to kill me. I need to kill myself. Now I need to die.'

I'd go binge-drinking with my mates on the weekend, connect with real friends on the Pokémon forum, then go on webcams and talk about sex with older guys and see their dicks. I was sexually experienced, but I'd never had a physical encounter. And not a single person at school knew. Not one. I was still this painfully beige, perfectionistic, disassociated kid.

I kept achieving, did the achieve-y things I was meant to. I was dux of Year 11, won the prizes for English, history, physics and geography. I was runner-up dux in Year 12, got the school's top ATAR, graduated, got into uni. From the outside, everything looked perfect. Charmed. More than perfect. On the inside, it was f**ken hell. I was thinking, 'Okay, I'll get married and have kids. And when I'm 50 or 60, the kids will have moved away, my wife will just die, and I'll be alone and I can finally be with guys.'

I had a brief, weird bottleneck of freedom and joy when I fled to Europe backpacking. I had to get out. I deferred uni, left the country the week after I turned eighteen, went to Covent Garden, the gay district of London, and finally did whatever I wanted. But after four months, my money ran out. That feeling, arriving back at Perth Airport, knowing I'd have to hide again, to squish myself back into my body? The worst. I remember thinking, as I walked towards the gate – the ones that slide open and people are waiting on the other side – 'As soon as I go through those doors, I'm finished.'

I planned to carry out suicide when I was nineteen. What stopped me, as I wrote the note, was that I couldn't say goodbye to my little sister. I was like, 'Oh my god, I can't do that to her. She needs me.' I couldn't hurt her, and I stopped writing and started crying.

Not long after, I was out of home, going to uni in Perth. I came out to my family when I had a boyfriend. It's harder to hide two people. We met in my creative writing class and spent six months flirting, which consisted of him being flirtatious and me saying, 'Mate, I'm straight. Leave me alone.' Eventually I texted back when I was drunk, and my cover was blown. He's my husband now.

My family were – mostly – fine. Same with close mates. Things tumbled into place once I was away and had a reason to say, 'I'm different.' I changed radically, and fast. Within a year, I'd shaved my hair into a mohawk. I'd been hiding my whole life – of course I did. I dyed it every colour. And it felt like, '*This* is what I want to look like: a f**ken *punk*.' It sends a message I don't have to verbalise.

I began standing up for myself, and a lot of people didn't stay around. Confronting toxic people and establishing and upholding some boundaries didn't necessarily go down well. There were arguments, screaming, gaslighting, ghosting. One person laughed and said, 'You finally grew some balls, did you? Took you long enough.' It felt glorious to be openly angry, though. When the dust settled, there were only a few people left, but it was the right decision. It gave me the space I needed to grow. People commented that I was a totally different person, and I was like, 'Yes, I'm stoked.'

I realised that you can be whoever you want, and that other people can't stop you. I became a gym junkie. I realised it doesn't matter if you're not great at footy – you can still play it. I play AFL socially with a gay team now, the Perth Hornets.

I was lonely my whole life, but, interestingly, *particularly* just after I came out. I thought I was the only gay bogan in the world. I rocked up to the gay 'scene' and didn't understand it. It felt even more performative than performing being straight. And I was like, 'Why are you pretending to be like this?' I was a total outsider. I'd been like, 'I'm out! And people finally get me.' But what happened was, 'I'm out!' And gay men were like, 'No ... you're a bogan,' which was bad. Dirty. Okay, but I'm *both*. I'm bogan *and* gay.

When *Invisible Boys* came out, I got tonnes of messages, men going, 'Oh my god. You understand me.' None from the gay scene. None of them visibly gay. They're guys in country towns or on farms, or in the city but they're truckers or labourers. There are *lots* of us. But we're not 'seen' because we don't fit the archetype.

'Gay' has become a cultural identity rather than just a sexual orientation. It comes with connotations. When I used to say 'I'm gay,' people would reply with all kinds of whack stuff – 'Let's go handbag shopping,' or something about drag queens – and I'd be like, no, you've completely misread me. I'm not dissing guys who love camp, but we have nothing in common beyond being men who like men. It's a trait I have, like being right-handed. It doesn't define me socially. I'm not 'gay'. I prefer 'homosexual' or 'same-sex attracted' or even 'rough trade'.

Some gay men grow up feminine and flamboyant, and they love it, and that's great. But if that's not you, if you're more aligned with traditional masculinity, like me, it's much harder to find your place in the world, and these men are more likely to want to kill themselves. Or do kill themselves. Or stay in the closet. Or marry women and go to public toilets to get off. Because they like men, but they're traditionally masculine guys, and that's not accepted – you don't exist.

I write about this because it needs to be written about. It would have been life-changing for me to read something like *Invisible Boys*. Just to know there were others out there like me. I was so isolated. My characters are unabashedly flawed, because everyone is. Some people don't like that, but it's not the point. Sure, Kade's unlikeable, but can't you understand why? You don't have to want to hang out with him to understand this kid is deserving of love. We all are.

We're not encouraged to show our bad side in public. It's not acceptable. I'm making the choice to undo years of damage by consciously putting that part of me on display. I grew up with, 'You must behave this way to be loved,' so I'm adamant about showing up as I am, even if I'm a bit rude or inappropriate. I don't like the performance of virtue. I did it for twenty years and it made me want to kill myself. Sometimes I'm nice, sometimes I'm an arsehole. That's okay. I can't live going, 'How do I maintain maximum likeability as an author?' I've given myself permission to be like Popeye – I yam what I yam.

A lot of gay guys message me about the way I present myself. We all grow up repressing a lot of things, and then compensate for what we see as bad or dirty about ourselves. But you've got to let yourself be those things too. They're fine. I'm also soft and sensitive, and the tough guy on the outside protects the soft guy on the inside. The more I let them both show up in the world, the more realised I am as a person.

It's not easy reinventing yourself from the ground up. It was lonely and exposing. But that's the process that developed my inner toughness. It's such relief to drop all pretence, be unapologetic and say, 'This is me, and I don't care what you think.' That strength is hard-won and lifesaving. My life is free of abuse, and I don't take anyone's shit, ever. I am the better for it.

If I'd grown up differently, without trauma, I'd definitely have fewer mental health issues. I live with anxiety, panic disorder and alcohol addiction. I had huge bouts of depression when I was younger. But ... if I hadn't grown up with adversity, I wouldn't be who I am now. I wouldn't be fully realised. I'd be *beige*. There are a lot of passive, scared and people-pleasing people, and I'd be one of them.

I'm pretty bold now. I've got big balls. I've got pluck. I can look someone in the eyes and tell them 'no'. I'm authentic. You just don't get that through an easy life. So if push came to shove, no, I wouldn't change anything. I survived it, it's made me who I am and I *like* who I am now. I'm peaceful in my own skin. I'm me.

Hardly any of my family are in my life now, which is a really hard thing to live with. I don't have any contact with my mother or my eldest brother. If people can't and won't change, then you've got to get away to keep yourself safe and mentally well. Our family is dysfunctional like this: other siblings have cut me off, or cut each other off, or cut the whole family off. The upshot is, I only interact with a couple of members of my immediate family now. We catch up, chat over coffee, play cards, watch the footy. It is what it is. I can be a grown-up and say that no family is perfect, that everyone's just doing the best they can with what they have, but it doesn't make it hurt any less to have grown up with such conditional and unstable relationships.

It's not that there weren't loving people in my life as a child, but I lacked support. Everything felt flimsy and conditional. I was on my own, fighting for myself. But I realise now that I did a good job. I looked after myself. My writing got me through. My stories kept me safe.

I wasn't writing dark, angry stuff at the time. Jake had lots of close, secure friendships: people who loved him, people who were always there. Everything I wrote had that feature. My characters had true friends who would never hurt them. I didn't have that, so I wrote what I needed.

It was always, 'I have to write, and I *will* write,' even from seven years old. There's never been a 'Maybe I'll give it up.' I knew I'd find a way and make it as a writer, because it's all I wanted. Well, writing and love. And I got both. Sometimes it feels like it took a long time. But I thought I'd be published at eight. Who does that? But then again, I did apply to be a town planner when I was ten ...

We went on a trip to Europe when I was a toddler. I guess that's when I became obsessed with maps and the world globe. I was fascinated by other countries and where we'd been. From very young, I was like, the world is not just Geraldton. The world is not just WA. The world is this huge, huge thing. And it's full of potential.

MEGAN WASHINGTON

There are a few words you could use to describe captivating singer-songwriter-artist Megan Washington: uncompromising, idiosyncratic and a little bit sweary. That's a large part of her charm – she's eloquent as all get-out, but uninhibited when it comes to mixing the four-letter words with the four-syllable ones. Why not? She pays little heed to what people think about her, these days.

Megan's self-proclaimed downfall at school was that she wanted to be liked too much, so put up with anything in the hope of being included. After years of unsuccessfully trying to please everybody else, including an early, short, highly successful career as a jazz singer covering classics and standards, she's now deliriously herself. Following her artistic nose and winning acclaim for her kooky, intelligent pop music.

After finally escaping school, Megan has the freedom to be disciplined, creatively motivated, and *romp*. Her first album, *I Believe You Liar*, went platinum in January 2011, two days before she and her band, the mononymous Washington, scored three songs in Triple J's Hottest 100. She won the ARIA award for Best Female Artist in 2010, then Breakthrough Songwriter of the Year in 2011, and was nominated for Best Female Artist and Best Pop Release in the same year. She followed up with *There There*, and *Batflowers* in 2020, described as 'pop music tearing at its own fabric'.

She's doing okay for the chubby, awkward girl who was transplanted from Papua New Guinea to Brisbane at age eleven, who nobody would sit next to, and who bribed kids with Chupa Chups to be her friends.

What was so hard was finding myself washed up in a place where reason and rationality had no existence. My tools didn't work. My intelligence didn't work. Because no one gave a flying rat's arse unless you were wearing Billabong or Quicksilver and had shiny blonde hair. The only thing that worked was being the girl everybody wants to know, which I wasn't.

As far as I'm concerned, my life began at eighteen. Okay, it started when I was born, but that part finished at eleven, when we moved from Papua New Guinea, and then from eleven to eighteen it was a whole effort to get the f**k out of there. In PNG everything was pretty good. I was happy. Then I went to a state school for a year in Brisbane. It was just awful. I didn't understand half the swear words, I didn't understand what they were calling me. I remember this girl said that my mother was a fat pig. I found that really disturbing, that even your parents weren't off limits.

When I was younger I was always very changey, a chameleonic kind of person, but I couldn't make it work at this school. All the kids were rough. *Rough*. And I'd never experienced physical danger before. One girl on the same softball team was really bad. I mean, I was sporty,

I wasn't a nerd. But she used to just throw the softball at me, aim it *into* me.

When I arrived at school in the morning people would throw their bags at me, and food at me, and call me bad names, and then we'd go into class. No one would sit with me because apparently I stank. And I wasn't to answer any questions, because that was to draw attention to myself, you know, so I never put my hand up because then everyone would look at me and remember that they hated me. So I'd get through class somehow, usually by ignoring everything, and then there'd be morning tea. I'd take my morning tea and find places to just walk, usually to the primary school area where the others weren't.

It was the psychology of it that was weird. Girls would say things like, 'My friend wants to ask you out on a date,' and then everyone would laugh. And that's really a mindf**k, as an eleven or twelve-year-old, because 'My friend wants to date you,' that's a positive statement, right? But when it's followed by laughter ... I remember feeling very confused most of the time. Not ever understanding what was going on. Entire mountains and valleys of all this subtext.

It made no sense, because a year before, in Papua New Guinea, I'd been totally normal. Normal! At that school everybody liked me, I had friends, we hung out and did stuff, and now I stank, and had a fat pig mother, and ... I couldn't understand. I kept wondering what it was about me that made me so repulsive or threatening.

I used to go to the library, and hang out with kids younger than me sometimes, and, because we lived close by, I ran away from school constantly. And I had to see a f**king counsellor, and it became *my* fault, because to deal with it my reaction was to become very angry and quite aggressive.

A year later I went to an all-girls private school, and the same thing happened. I thought once I went to a different school it would be okay, but when I got to Year 8 it was all f**ked again. The difference was the bullying was now no body, all brain.

I was short and chubby and awkward and had braces, but I was in the popular girl group. I can see now I was only there as the comic relief, they kept me in the group for sport. They all had names like Cheryl and Candace and Vanessa, and at the time I thought they were my friends. But at lunchtime they'd sit with me in a circle and say something like, 'We really need to talk to you about your appearance.' And they'd talk about how when I didn't shave my legs it was disgusting. And how I was getting pimples, and also a little bit fat, and not in a kind way. I mean, that's not kind.

Once, when we were in Year 10, they said, 'There's a party on Friday, everybody's going, you should come,' all welcoming and warm, and emailed or texted me the address. So, on Friday, they were like, 'We'll see you tonight, yeah, bye, yeah,' and I came home from school, and had a shower, and got all dressed up, and I got my dad to drive me. I think he left work early so he could drive me. And ... the address was just a fish and chip shop, a gap between houses, something. Then it was just me and dad driving back, in silence.

The dumb thing was I wanted to stay in that group. I don't know why, but I did. I guess I thought it was better to be the worst house in the best street. I'd rather be in this cool group no matter what.

My undoing was that I had this desperate, fundamental urge to be liked. If I'd been happy to mind my own business, to adopt the loser crown and just wear it, I would have avoided a lot of the shit. After a while I did settle into this area of ... well, I used to stop at the servo and buy lollies and share them all the time, just to have a friend.

I was totally unwilling to accept that people didn't like me. They thought I was 'X, Y, Z,' and I was like, 'I'm not! I'm not! I'm not! I'll show you! I'll show you! I'll show you!' I couldn't just say, 'I'll only know you for the next five years, and then I'll never see you again,' because when you're at school, five years is an *eternity*.

I used to *dread* Mondays. I remember thinking that I would prefer to die, actually physically die, than go back to school next year. I would rather have a life-threatening illness and be in hospital for a year, than go back there. I just hated it all. Every minute of it. I lived in the sick bay. It's a wonder I passed half my classes. The nurses were the most compassionate people in the whole school. They knew. They'd say, 'Have a Panadol and a lie-down, darling,' and they might even slip you a *Women's Weekly* under the pillows.

The only lucky thing was that I had an extracurricular life, my dancing. There was no one at ballet school from my real school, so I could be myself there. And I was good, and in ballet class that's the only thing that matters. I spent more and more hours there, and I'd leave school early to have private lessons.

I asked my parents a thousand times to take me out of that school. I'd rather be nowhere than somewhere shit – you know how shit coffee is worse than no coffee? I tried so many things. My first plan was that if I did well academically, people would like me, and it became all about hiding in the library the whole time. That didn't work, and besides, I'm an extrovert and I got bored.

The next way I tried to come back from being so ostracised, from being so deeply unhappy, lonely and sad, was by being outrageous – so naughty, so bad, that you got respect that way. I was Charlie Chaplin with a bad attitude. The most slovenly dressed, tough, note-passing, joke-telling, face-pulling, slapstick, loud, you name it. It kind of worked because people knew who I was, but they still didn't like me.

So I became a terror. A really naughty kid. I was suspended a hundred times. I'd not turn up to my exam because it was more dramatic not to go. I got lots of detentions. One teacher used to pick fights with me in class. Every day. For like two terms. Then one day we got into an argument, it escalated, it got more and more heated, she threw a whiteboard eraser at my head, so I just picked up a chair and put a crack in the whiteboard.

That was the start of the fourth term in Year 10, and the school said, 'Don't come back for the rest of the term.' I had eight weeks off, and they just sent me the exams at home. Mum had a lot of trouble getting me into another school because they were like, 'We don't want her.' Mum had to *beg* this woman at another school who eventually said, 'We'll give her a term and we'll see what happens.'

And then I went to a new school and it was fine. It was full of nerds, every other reject from every other school. It had a performing arts bent, I had a complete shift, and my dancing became my focus.

But I'm grateful for my background now. I'm glad that I experienced the worst, worst, worst when I was thirteen, fourteen, fifteen, because nothing I encounter will ever be as bad. Being bullied has given me tools. Hard-won, amazing tools.

I learned that compromising doesn't work. I'm comfortable making the hard choices and not being part of any institution. The advantage, when you've never been invited to be part of anything, is I don't give a toss who likes me or who doesn't. People who blog about me and say, 'She's this and she's that and why is she wearing safety glasses?'

It doesn't bother me at all. You put no stock in the things that the general population care about. I could not give a flying rat's arse about tit implants or any of that stuff. I'm comfortable with looking like a nine-year-old boy, because that's how I look.

It's really affected how I do business. I only hire, or work with, people I genuinely like or respect, and who like and respect me. I'd never go with a label or manager who had something over me, or bullied me, or tried to influence me in any way. I don't need to make friends that I don't want. I emit a different frequency to most people. A frequency that is 'whatever'. It's made me quite unsentimental. Pragmatic. You know, 'I'm going to have to fire you. Sorry about that.'

I think being bullied gives you power, because it steels you. It forges you at a really early age, and it makes you strong and hard and ready. I don't know if I could do what I do now, in the fashion I'm doing it – which is with no time, no money, no nothing – if I didn't have a steeliness.

And I've learned about power itself, because I know how much power I gave to those people. I gave them everything. So I know how much power there is to be had. It's a currency and I understand how humans deal in it.

And it forces you to *really* know yourself. It forces you. I remember I used to talk to myself, because, like, you need to talk through what's happening, and you don't have any friends. So I really got to know myself, because I talked to myself all the time.

I would undramatise everything that happened: take the emotion out and go, 'It was just a physical punch in my physical face, it doesn't mean anything.' Or, 'It was just a name, and that name is just two words, and the words have four letters each, which come from the

Greek root, blah blah.' I'd totally abstract the event, which made it dealable. That way of thinking about things has really influenced me, the ability to compartmentalise every terrifying situation into something that can't hurt me.

The best thing was when I suddenly realised I wasn't ugly – it was the most liberating thing in the whole world. I'd believed it for a very, very long time, and then it was, 'I'm not ugly! I don't smell! In fact, I smell great!' I can really appreciate my youth now. I'm 24, and I look pretty good. It's a great feeling, to be able to own myself. Everything that I am, is just where I want to be, and I don't do a single thing that I don't want to do.

I do think being bullied makes you special. You don't get to join in, so it makes you a very idiosyncratic human being, very distinctive. You're special because you really have no other option, and it's also why you get singled out. I learned to embrace my uniqueness, and cultivate, develop and explore it.

The irony, the *irony*, is that the majority of people who are admired and respected in the world, probably came from this kind of background. All the cool kids go out and get drunk, and go to gigs, and parties, and music festivals, and have a great time. And the nerds, the people who were ostracised and unpopular, are at home listening to records, reading books, playing guitar, engorging themselves on culture, and then, bam, they're Tame Impala, they're massive, and all the cool kids are going to go see them. I never went to anything cool, I was always at home reading books and writing songs about my feelings. The first time I went to a Big Day Out, I was 23 and playing at it!

If you look around at the individuals that people like and follow, it's always the people who are so not normal. People like Lady Gaga and Paul Capsis and Oprah. They're not Joe and Mary Average, they're unusual, a rare species of human, and that's why people gravitate towards them. The most individual people are the most interesting and they're the ones who never fitted in. A lot of people have really dull lives, and I know, because all the bitches found me on Facebook last year and tried to friend me, and they're all working at their dad's plumbing firm, or married and living in the 'burbs.

Look, if you spend most of your school years going out and doing what everybody else does, you'll always do what everybody else does. I'm so glad I didn't peak at high school. I don't want to peak. Not until I'm 65. I'll be writing musicals for Broadway or other cool shit. I'm going to make *my* music, make *my* art, write my pieces, be *me*. It can be difficult to be distinctive, to own that, but when it's difficult then I think, well, it's all I've got. Me.

ANNIE
LOUEY

Chinese-Australian comic Annie Louey lives by a few credos. She responds poorly to women being told they can't do things, and will have a crack at anything that's considered off limits because of her gender. She lives life as though it's as short as a lit bomb fuse, and she is ever up for a challenge, whether it's sampling 150 unique flavours of potato chip or joining the Australian Army Cadets in Year 9.

A stand-out talent in Australia's rising tide of compelling and diverse comedians, Melbourne-born Annie was a quirky, studious kid in search of top grades and ways to fit in. Humour was her release valve as she railed against the constricting expectations of her traditional Chinese parents, racism at school and cultural expectations of what was considered appropriate for a girl (spoiler: nothing she found of interest).

Annie's life changed at sixteen when rebellion led her to a training camp and an accident which left her face severely burned and her mental health in a deep dive to depression and anxiety. But she also emerged post-accident with a blazing determination not to hold herself back and three months of accumulated inspiration, having watched an entire Blockbuster store's worth of stand-up comedy DVD hires. These days Annie is a stand-up comic with an eye on her own mortality, as well as a trained journalist, a celebrant, a TV presenter on ABC's *China Tonight* and Channel 10's *The Project*, and a scriptwriter. She would not change a thing.

At primary school, people would say I was 'weird', even my friends. But I took it in my stride and saw it as a positive. I still do. I was also the high-achieving teacher's pet, the dorky kid who sucked up a lot. I'd probably self-identify these days as a nerd. I wasn't cool, but I'd be voted house captain. I got top marks and strived to be the best. Some of it was because of my parents pushing me to make a better life, but I quite enjoyed primary school. I'd give teachers gifts and write them cards for no reason. Like, when I first got a printer, the first thing I did was print Christmas cards for the teachers.

I sucked up to teachers because I didn't have a core, consistent friendship group. My friends were always leaving or changing schools, so the teachers were my constant. The school was very multicultural – languages included Turkish, Arabic and Italian – and there were refugee kids and Lebanese, Syrian and Yugoslav kids. A lot of my friends were Indonesian. Their parents would be in Melbourne to study their master's degrees, and then they'd move back to their countries. I had *cycles* of friends where we'd become really close and then I'd have to say goodbye.

We lived in Brunswick, where there weren't many Chinese families, so I was always the odd one out. I was desperate to fit in. I was jealous of the Lebanese kids with their bunches of siblings and cousins and their pita and Nutella for lunch. I also wanted to be as Aussie as possible. I mean, everyone did. All I wished for was a sandwich, but I always had a hot lunch. There was only one other kid, an Indian boy, who had hot lunches, and he was ostracised for it. Mum attempted to Australianise, but it was all wrong: her sandwiches were massive and soggy, with chunks of chicken breast and tomato and plastic cheese and tomato sauce. I could only eat a bit of them before I had to throw them out.

I was even proud to be a 'banana' at one point – you know, yellow on the outside and white on the inside? And now I'm like, 'What the hell?' I had internalised racism for sure. Only recently I had to get over my dislike of the Chinese accent. I found it so hard to listen to. I don't 'hear' it now, and I'm far less judgemental. I mean, they know how to speak multiple languages – I don't.

I got the eye-pulling and 'ching chong Chinaman' stuff from the other kids. I'd tell Dad, and he'd joke and say, 'I'll go and beat them up for you.' Not that he ever would. But it reminded him that nothing had changed. Dad's side of the family came from China during the gold rush, from the 1850s onwards. They set up a vegetable farm in Coleraine, near the border of South Australia, and my grandparents had a milk bar there where Dad learned English from interacting with customers, but he was never fluent. My generation was the first where someone in the family was born here. In the White Australia policy days, they weren't allowed to bring their wives over because Australia didn't want Chinese families to live here, essentially. When the sons in our family came of age in China, they'd be sent for and put to work in the business. Awareness of racism in Australia was part of my upbringing.

I pushed back against my parents a *lot*. There was a 35-year age difference between Mum and Dad, and 64 years between me and Dad. *Totally* different generations. We were always going to butt heads. Mum was 28 when she came to Australia a year before I was born. She and Dad had been introduced by Dad's mother, who had matchmade them back in her village. Mum was raised traditionally and followed Dad's advice on everything.

Dad held very old-school views on girls' behaviour. I loved climbing on monkey bars, and was always covered in bruises and getting injured. He'd scold me, saying, 'That's not very ladylike.' It was a constant refrain of, 'You can't do these things because you're a girl.' The double standards made me furious and I constantly rebelled. It's probably why I gravitate towards anything if 'women can't do it'. Stand-up's male dominated. So is cycling. If you say I can't do something, I'll give it a crack.

It was a possessive mindset: the traditional belief that you keep girls home and protect them. In my first week at primary school, a little boy invited me to his sixth birthday party, and it was, 'No, it's a boy's house.' It never let up. 'Can I go to the movies with friends?' 'No.' 'Can I go shopping?' 'No.' 'Can we not name my baby sister "Anna" because it's basically my name?' 'No.' Dad took great offence at that one. It didn't take much to trigger a screaming match, particularly once I was in my emo phase, slamming doors, playing loud music and crying into my pillow. Eventually I stopped asking and started just 'doing'.

There's a photo from when I was little: I was wearing Dad's clothes and parodying him, pointing my finger like, 'Don't do that.' I always used humour to vent frustration about things outside of my control. Laughing was also how I'd bond with friends at school. I'd write parodies of fairytales at recess and lunchtime, practise them with my friendship group – as they left the school, I'd bring others in – and they'd let us perform at assemblies. My parents always said, 'Oh, she's so cute,' and probably thought it was a phase, but I guess I was always a writer and performer. In high school I took it seriously and wanted to take classes. That created tension. I always had to prioritise, to choose what was really worth the fight, and the anti-authoritarian part of me came out. My parents were so against absolutely everything I wanted that I thought, 'What's the worst I can do? Probably drama. Yeah, let's do that.'

I just wanted to live my own life and not be told 'no' to everything, which is how I ended up in the Australian Army Cadets in Year 9. There was a strong camping and outdoors element, and Dad didn't take us on holidays, so I thought I'd enjoy it. And I did enjoy it, being one with nature and peeing in the bush! You learned first aid and radio skills and fire-starting – I think I nailed that one – and how to cook outdoors and navigate.

We did lots of training. Monday afternoons and evenings were committed to marching on the oval, getting rained on and yelled at. So much marching. Mum and Dad were very against it. They'd come from a communist regime specifically to a free country where you didn't have to do that stuff. I'd be practising march steps in our living room and polishing brass belts. The more they hated it, the more I wanted to push back and get involved.

By Year 10, I'd advanced to the rank of lance corporal and was leading a group of five for winter camp, where you're roughing it for a week. We were preparing a survival dinner, where they give you food and utensils but not everything you need. I was peeling a pumpkin with one of the kids' pocket knives, which wasn't the right tool but all I could find, and it felt kind of wrong, but I was like, 'Nah, let's just keep going.' I learned to trust my gut after that.

The knife slipped and sliced my middle finger. There was a lot of blood. I trekked around trying to locate the first-aid kit, *and a*n older cadet said, 'Just stand here and relax. We'll find it.' And that's when I blacked out and fell face-first into the campfire that I'd started.

I have no memory of falling in, which is probably for the best. I was only in there for seconds – they pulled me out straight away – but the coals were incredibly hot and caused severe burns to my face and neck. When I woke, I could smell burnt hair, and my friend Georgia was clearly trying to hold it together. She said, 'Don't worry, you're going to be gorgeous again in no time.' And I was a self-conscious teenager, so did not think I was 'gorgeous' in the first place, and I'm like, 'Ah, I really f**ked this up. Like, what is happening?'

I had first-, second- and third-degree burns to about ten per cent of my body. Third-degree burns are called 'full thickness' now, meaning all the nerves are damaged. They're the hardest to heal, and that's what I had around my jaw. My left eye was glued shut from the swelling, and the worst-case scenario was that I'd lost sight in that eye. It was terrifying.

I could only mumble because my lips were super swollen, my skin was red and I couldn't see out of my left eye. So I'm like, 'Yeah, this must be really bad.' They cut my uniform off at Northern Hospital Epping, and my scars are still shaped like the V-neck I was wearing. So that's always a reminder. I didn't know what I looked like at this point, but later on the nurses said they couldn't tell what ethnicity I was. They were surprised when a Chinese family rocked up.

I was kind of surprised too. I'd convinced myself they wouldn't come. Dad didn't drive at night and rarely picked me up from things, and to them the hospital was in the middle of nowhere. I thought I'd get a taxi home when I was better. But they figured it out, and my aunt came too, and she was *wailing*, screaming her head off at the sight of me.

I was in hospital for two weeks and off school for three months, and I fell into a very deep depression. If I could have dropped out of school completely, I would have. I went from being an extroverted kid who made friends easily to not wanting to go out in public, not wanting to meet people and hating having my photograph taken. I couldn't bear to be noticed or looked at or asked questions. I turned inwards. I was so lucky not to lose my eyesight or need skin grafts, but it sucked that the damage was on such a visible part of my body.

My skin tried to regenerate too quickly. It went, 'Let's repair this,' and went overboard. My chin grew out of control so that half of it was sticking out, and I had lots of steroid injections to flatten it. I lost an entire eyebrow and a patch of hair. I wore compression garments when I was sleeping. They make you look like you're about to rob a bank, with only eye, nose and mouth holes, and I went through a couple of dozen of those. I'd wake with silicon sheets stuck to my face. I had to keep my skin hydrated with moisturiser, so my face was very shiny, bright red and bandaged for months. There was a lot of pain.

I did not want to live. Every morning I'd wake up and remember what had happened. Every day I wished so badly to go to sleep and wake up with someone else's life. I didn't care whose, so long as it wasn't mine. I was desperate for a different body that hadn't been burned. The damage was cosmetic in the end, like I'm not physically hindered, but the setbacks to mental health are much harder to measure.

I went to see the school counsellor, and after a couple of sessions they said I was pretty positive and didn't need to go back. But it was all put on. I just wanted to be normal so much that I faked it. I didn't want to address it with friends; I didn't want to talk about it. 'Oh, it didn't affect me! I'm fine!'

Any time I had to talk about it, I'd get a huge rush of adrenalin. Going out in public made me anxious, and I had a fight-or-flight response whenever a stranger looked at me or asked a question, which happened a lot. I hated it. I'm still self-conscious. Even today I overthink what angle I'm being seen from, where I'm sitting when I talk to strangers. It's a form of body dysmorphia, because I sometimes think I look the way I did when I was freshly burned.

I became very reliant on make-up. I realised I could cover it up. 'If it's less red, people will ask fewer questions!' I became obsessed with appearing normal. I've wasted so much time trying to perfect my skin before leaving the house. Friends and family are like, 'No one cares; no one can tell,' but they can't see how difficult it is. I'm getting better. I'm in an industry where I audition a lot and I'm looked at very closely, so I set myself little challenges, to go out with no make-up, or with my hair up.

I assumed there was a finishing line, a point when I would be recovered. I set goals. 'Maybe I'll look normal for the Year 11 formal.' And then, 'Maybe next year when I graduate.' And ten plus years later I'm still not 'recovered', but it's not that bad now. There's no sensation in parts of my face and one side of my face doesn't look like the other. The same goes for my ears, so I don't like putting my hair up. There's some scarring. Part of the skin next to my eye is a different colour. But it's better to know there's no 'finish line'. You just have to be satisfied.

I don't regret any of those experiences, though, because they've shaped me and allowed me to get the successes I've had. If I could go back and do it all again, let's face it, I would. It's just in my nature. If your parents are going to say no to everything, what are you going to do? You can't live. So, I would still choose to join that program, and I'd still do what I did. After my accident, the school shut the program down, saying girls couldn't to do cadets anymore. It made me really angry. I wrote and asked them not to but they ignored it.

The accident freed me up in some ways. It made me want to live outside the box even more. I used to veer towards self-doubt and anxiety, and there's no way would I have gathered the confidence to do stand-up that way. But during those three months off school, all I did was watch stand-up comedy on DVD. I cleaned out the local Blockbuster. And I thought, 'This is *good*. I really want to do this.' I'd done improvisation at school in Year 7, and thought of comedy as a bucket-list item, but it became an imperative: 'I could have died. I'd better get on with it.' I entered Melbourne International Comedy Festival's Class Clowns competition for high-school students that year, and performed material about being Chinese with my face bandaged.

My mental state seesawed between, 'I want to die. Why did this happen to me?' and, 'Wow, I could have died. I'd better live!' I wanted to do everything I thought I might miss out on. Realising you could have died is motivating. Even now, I feel like I'm on bonus time and there are no rules.

My sense of humour got me through. Performing gave me control back from being stared at. It was the whole, 'Oh, take a picture, it'll last longer' thing. I thought, 'If you're going to look at me, I want there to be a reason, and for it to be on my terms. I'll be on stage for seven minutes – that's when you can look.' Comedy gave me a powerful tool to shine the light only where I wanted it. I could deflect attention, I could make fun of others, I could make fun of myself. One time back at school, the heater was up high in the classroom and a friend was overheating. 'Oh, my god,' she said. 'It feels like my face is on fire.' And I'm like, 'You're telling me.'

It felt so much better to laugh. I always found it easier to say something funny than something serious, and it escalated. I was cracking jokes, just wanting to talk shit with my friends. I was talking too much, distracting the others, and the teachers disapproved. But I felt like I had seen the light! 'I could have died! Who gives a shit if I talk too much? Who's with me?' And when I *was* ready to talk about it all, stand-up was the natural place. It was therapy before I knew you could actually just go to therapy.

My parents, though, did not want to talk about it. They thought problems related to mental health meant you were 'mental'. There was a lot of blame – 'We told you not to do this, we didn't approve of you doing this, and you went and did it anyway' – and I didn't go to family gatherings for at least six months. There's shame and stigma about disability and burns survivors in Chinese culture. You don't talk about it, and you hide away. I have more insight into my childhood now. There's intergenerational trauma there: Dad narrowly missed being killed by Japanese soldiers as a kid, Mum grew up in a famine during the Great Leap Forward. They suppressed a lot. The school gave me a psychologist's number, but it was easier to bin it than stir up those conversations. When I tell Mum I'm anxious or depressed, she still says, 'Don't think rubbish,' and, 'Think good things.'

But the anxiety and depression help me a lot, too. It's the same part of my brain that produces jokes, and thinking differently to other people is a great benefit. It's a powerful brain, and the overthinking helps. The inner dialogue is where all the jokes come from. It's essential for my comedy to have time for thinking.

I'm passionate now about wanting equality and creating spaces that are free of judgement. As a woman, a person of colour and someone with a facial difference, there are lots of places I haven't been welcome in. Now I'm producing comedy rooms and mentoring, making spaces I wish I'd had. My work is rewarding.

I've learned that something negative can turn into a positive – you just don't know when. I've learned that it's so important to have support. There's a lot I admired about Dad: his ability to crack a joke and tell a story, his connection to community. When he passed away, family became more important; we're all closer now. My parents' advice was to be the best and try your hardest, and I still follow that. I take Mum to gigs now, the big ones, and I think she's proud. I mean, she still says, 'I gave you perfect skin as a baby and you ruined it,' and compares me to people who are buying houses and having children, but I'm not too fussed. I've learned that I can't please everybody. I see people living that way and I won't do it.

I deeply understand that your time is limited, and I value that perspective. I worked at a funeral home for a while, which helped with the thoughts I sometimes still have of not wanting to be here by giving me perspective. There's no 'right' way to live your life. I'm doing what I love; I'm on the right track.

I could have died, so nothing is to be expected of me. I make deliberate choices. I assess myself every day and check in with myself every night: 'Is what I did today what I want to do? Did it align with my values? Am I doing what I love?' Then I ask myself, 'Would I be happy if I died in my sleep?' And most days, I'm pretty good.

COREY TUTT

Sometimes you have to reject the narrative you're offered to get the life you want. No one knows this better than Sydney-based Corey Tutt, proud (very proud) Kamilaroi man formerly from Illawarra in NSW and founder and CEO of DeadlyScience, a charity that supplies science books and STEM resources to remote schools. Corey grew up fighting: to not have his food or money nicked, to not be assaulted, to not be abducted, to understand his family's intergenerational trauma, to process deaths and grief, to learn, to be loved and – always – to not be underestimated.

A keen natural scientist and smart human, Corey's big dream was to be a zookeeper. As an Aboriginal kid, it was assumed he was heading for jail or worse. He confounded expectations and found his purpose: to challenge the presumption that Indigenous kids can only aspire to sport or art and to inspire a generation of deadly scientists. Corey's mission is to create equity in education, normalise science as a pathway and decolonise the lab coat. Books and mentors changed *his* life, and now he's paying it forward.

Corey was the 2020 NSW Young Australian of the Year, the Sydney Science Festival's 2021 Ambassador and the 2019 CSIRO STEM Champion Award winner, is Chair of the NSW Executive Committee for National Science Week and Inspiring Australia, and has won a Eureka Prize. His children's book, *The First Scientists*, centres First Nations people as innovators and inventors; Corey's changing the narrative again, rewriting Aboriginal and Torres Strait Islander children's futures to be limitless.

I had one goal as a kid: I dreamed of being a zookeeper. I was always outdoors, catching and picking up reptiles and telling people about them. We moved around – at times I missed school – and I'd try to make new friends by doing snake and lizard shows.

My energy went into looking at animals and reading, learning from real life. I was a good rugby-league player, could have gone on with it if I'd applied myself more. Sometimes I'd be really focused and score heaps of tries, and then I'd be looking at an eagle and the ball would go straight past me.

Other kids were into bodyboarding, so I had a board, and I'd pretend I was bodyboarding to be cool. But I was looking at the fish on the reef, you know? I was reared on Harry Butler tapes – I wanted to be him. A famous herpetologist! My poppy gave me my first book, *Australian Reptiles in Colour*, from, like, 1984, so it was pretty worn-out by the time it got to me. But it meant everything. It taught me to read and developed my interest in wildlife and animals. Poppy Walford was the best natural scientist I ever knew, and he was illiterate.

My mum and my dad, who was a Gomaroi man, separated when I was two. Mum was very fearful of him; there was some domestic violence there. She was worried he'd abduct us. My sister and I grew up being fearful of him too, and we weren't allowed to go out and play in our front yard. I remember being terrified when a Christmas card he'd signed arrived on our doorstep.

She's a good person, my mum. She tried her absolute best, but her trauma certainly affected my sister and me growing up. We spent the first few years of my life sharing a mattress, and the barriers of being a single parent with trauma kept Mum from being her best. It wasn't always easy. She's doing well now, and I'm proud of her.

My older sister played a huge role looking after me as a child – she helped raise me. She'd get my lunch ready for school, was making me eggs when she was twelve. I spent 99 per cent of my time with her. If we had loose change, she'd buy us chips and gravy from the fish and chip shop.

I was a little brown kid, very dark because I was always outside. My sister's dad was white, and I wasn't welcome in her grandparents' house because I was half-Aboriginal. I had to sit in the car while Mum visited. Other members of the family could be racist too. They'd say things like, 'Aboriginals break into houses.' Little did I know, my mum was Aboriginal herself.

I think maybe she *suspected*, but there were a lot of lies told in our family to cover up abuse, shame, Aboriginal heritage. There was a lot of intergenerational trauma. Nothing made sense. My dad's other children looked whiter than me, and I was the only one with Aboriginal features. My sister was fair because we had different dads, but otherwise we looked the same. Mum was told she had a white father. This was proven to be incorrect: her father was Kamilaroi.

I was my pop's favourite grandchild by far. He loved a joke, would send a birthday card every year with $5 in there, and it would be a girl's card, Bratz or Barbie themed. He looked out for me. He'd call me 'Blackie' and other racist names when I was a kid to teach me not to worry about it. He said, 'You're going to get this when you're older, and you need to get used to it.' He was right. When I got called 'half-caste' or 'not black enough', it was water off a duck's back.

The early years of Bulli primary school were pretty easy. It was fun until I was nearly eight. Mum was finally letting me walk to school because I'd begged her for weeks. These two girls lived across the road from us, and I was cheeky. We'd run down opposite sides of the road and poke our tongues out and stick our fingers up at each other, and then run and meet at the school gates. We did that for a couple of months, and would hang out at recess and lunch.

This particular day, I played chicken outside the school gates. There was a car a way off, a green Commodore, and I ran onto the road and back – there was plenty of time. Then the little man went green and the girls started crossing the road. I was poking fun and they were laughing, and then I saw the car drive right into them. The mechanic from across the road ran and literally threw me over the fence, told me to piss off. But I knew she was dead from the moment it happened, from when she got hit. I was two metres away. I was featured in the local newspaper for weeks afterwards, and I relived the accident throughout my childhood.

I'd say I had PTSD from the accident; in fact, I'd say I still do. It was the early 2000s, so no one understood it. Mum pulled me out of school a couple of months afterwards because I couldn't do my work. Not one teacher asked if I was okay. They didn't get that my friend was killed in front of me. I was told not to speak about it. I was told that if I said I'd witnessed something, they'd take me away and put me in a home.

It made me empathetic, though. I probably always was, but it made me see how fleeting life was. It made me want to be a good person. After the accident, I picked some flowers and put them on the doorstep of the old woman who'd driven the car. People hated her. You don't hit two eight-year-olds and kill one of them without people hating you. But she didn't mean to. It was just a terrible accident. Sometimes ... life just sucks.

I didn't spend my childhood up till then being a really caring person. I was a very tough kid. I grew up fighting other kids, other people, who were trying to take my money or my lunch or harm me. I would have to fight people off. My cousins were rough and I got beaten up multiple times.

Mum put me through boxing as well as footy, so I was strong – small, but feisty, and I wouldn't back down. One time there were four guys who wanted my bike. They thought it was cool. It was a cheapo girl's bike from Kmart, which we'd bought from a girl up the road. I'd scraped the pink paint off and spray-painted it all murally. It *did* look cool. I beat them in the fight because I just fought more than they did. I wanted to keep my bike.

My life was chaotic. So much was happening.

If it wasn't for that empathy I found, I don't know where I'd have ended up, to be honest. I always had to be ready to fight, and I'd be on edge, worried my dad was going to turn up. Not that he did. I've spoken on the phone to Dad twice since I was two. He's like, 'I've got a lot of kids. Two of them are dead. I don't need another one.' That's what he said. It is what it is.

I'm still tough now, but I don't fight. My mum, my pop, my sister all taught me never to go out of your way to hurt anyone. I was playing rugby recently and some guy on the sideline called me a 'half-caste c**t'. That hurt – I haven't heard that in years. But I couldn't clobber him because I was Young Australian of the Year. If I'd hit him, it would have been in the *Daily Mail* ...

I was good academically at high school, especially at history and English. Poppy said to always try your best, and I put 110 per cent into everything. But at school, as an Aboriginal kid you only get praise for being good at sport. Schoolwork wasn't encouraged. Each year, I worked really hard at school and I'd wait with bated breath, but the only awards I got were for footy.

One teacher found out I was distantly related to a Port Adelaide player and made me captain of the AFL team. I'd never played AFL and I sucked at it. I'm fast and stuff, so I could weave, do some magic, but I couldn't kick a ball straight. I'd score 17 points, and that would be 17 behinds. It's like, dude, you should not be picking me in this team just because I'm Indigenous. Let alone as captain.

I've always been pretty smart. When I was fifteen, the NSW Department of Education brought in a secure login to stop kids accessing sites like YouTube and Myspace at school. One of my reptile sites was banned so I was annoyed. I'm not a computer guy, but I was focused. I worked out that the teacher's password was her husband's name and his birthday, which wasn't a very safe password, but, you know, each to their own. This was the one time I did anything wrong, by the way. I worked really hard at school.

I made myself a casual teacher account and I could log in and give my mates unlimited access. Then kids from other schools offered me money to get around *their* systems. I accessed tests and test results, and got band 6s in my Year 10 certificate because I knew all the answers. I was the most popular kid in school for a couple of weeks until someone got caught by the deputy principal. I showed the deputy how I did it and helped safeguard the system, and got off with afternoon detentions. It wasn't very honest, but it was fun.

At the end of Year 9, you're asked to think about what you want to do with your life and I definitely thought about it. We had to take three options to the careers advisor in Year 10, and I wrote down 'zookeeper', 'adventure documenter' and 'sports commentator', 'cause I knew I could talk well, and I thought it could finance the other two. The careers advisor said, 'That's not going to happen. You've got three options. You're going to leave school and get a trade, leave school and go to prison, or leave school and die.'

The Indigenous programs were demeaning. On Monday afternoons, instead of studying science or maths, all the Aboriginal kids were loaded onto a bus and driven to Wollongong Uni to do the Aboriginal cultural program. There wasn't any academic value to it. Like, wouldn't it have been good for us to be taking in science or maths?

The one good thing about the program was that there were mentors, and I met Paul Sinclair, an Aboriginal man working as an arachnid keeper at Taronga Zoo, living my dream! I told him what the careers advisor said, that I couldn't go to university or study zoology or be a zookeeper. Paul had never been to uni, hadn't finished Year 12 and just volunteered to get into zookeeping. It was a huge deal to know there was another path.

So at sixteen, I found a wildlife sanctuary to volunteer at, Roo

Gully in WA. I took a couple of jobs and put $50 a night into a Milo can until I'd saved $1000 to get there. While I was there, I studied my Cert II in Animal Studies by correspondence, and got accepted to do my Captive Animals Cert III at Nowra Animal Park. I could not believe it. On my first day at Nowra, the head zookeeper told me not to be so keen and sent me to shovel animal poo. I didn't care. I was just excited to be in with some camels. He also called me a 'retard' for picking up some gum leaves the wrong way. He was difficult to work with – when I first started doing reptile shows, he'd interrupt in front of everyone to tell me I was doing a bad job.

But I loved it. I had this little camcorder, so on my lunchbreak I'd record videos of myself catching a water dragon or a dragon fly or a cicada. I'd bring a handline, catch a freshwater bass and talk about it. That was me living my dream as a seventeen-year-old.

When the owner gave me a casual job and made me a paid zookeeper, he did not understand what it meant to me, how I was an Aboriginal kid who'd dreamed of that day my whole life. I was so proud. When he gave me my shirt, I put it straight on, didn't take it off for, like, two days. I kept it until last year. It looked like Swiss cheese – so many holes.

It was easily the best job and worst job I've ever had. I thrived off it, giving the reptile shows, connecting people to the animals. It was also, yeah, a bit *Tiger King*. I'd pick up wild snakes to show the public, and one time my thigh was gored by a wild pig we had in a pen. I lost a lot of blood, had twelve stitches and was back to work the next day.

I'd open up the gates for Aboriginal people in Nowra and just let them in. I'd turn a blind eye and let my mates pull up boats along the river. I'd probably still be there, to be honest, but I'd become best mates with another volunteer there. He didn't stay long – they didn't keep him on – but we had a grand plan. I was moving out of home and we were going to move in together to a house in Bomaderry. It was all set. And then he hanged himself. That was pretty much me done.

I was numb. I lost the joy of the job. I chased it, doing risky things like jumping in the lace monitor pit and pulling one out. But I didn't care. If I'd got bitten by a snake, if the crocodile had killed me, I would not have cared. My friends called me 'Wild Turkey' because I'd drink a whole bottle of Wild Turkey on a weekend. I was not prepared for life. I didn't get the skills you need to deal with crisis.

Eventually my stepdad showed me an ad he'd found for an alpaca handler job, and I went, the hell with it; at least there's travel. I ended up shearing with this guy James Dixon for a couple of years. He probably gets embarrassed by me saying it, but he saved my life. I'd never had a real role model before, someone I could look up to and say, yeah, that's where I can go. I was nineteen, I'd just lost my best friend and I did not have a good outlook on life. He was highly educated, had studied chemical engineering, listened to the Spice Girls and was twenty years older than me. Not the type of person I would normally hang with. But I was forced to talk to him because we'd be in the car together for twelve hours one day and then spend sixteen hours the next day together in a shearing shed. He became my unofficial counsellor. He listened and made me feel valued as a person, was there for me rain, hail or shine.

I always had a love of learning but he forced me to educate myself. I studied animal technology, worked at the RSPCA and the Animal Welfare League, and then got a job as a research assistant at the University of Sydney. Working in the labs was a good job, but boring.

There were only so many standard operating procedures I could write. It was like, you start at six, finish at two, give a couple of injections to a couple of rats. I had spare time. I thought, well, I'll go volunteer.

I joined the AIME program, the same program I'd met Paul at, and I became a mentor to all these kids. Kids like me, who don't get opportunities. No one had told *me* I could be a scientist, and I didn't want them to feel they weren't capable, that they couldn't follow a dream other than sport or arts. I brought them into the animal labs, kitted them up in gowns, showed them what the researchers were doing. Those kids were smarter than me, their ceiling was higher. I wanted them to know they could do it. I realised that I wasn't meeting other Aboriginal people working in STEM and I wanted to change that.

I contacted some remote schools. They had plenty of footballs, but not many books, not many science resources. One school only had fifteen books in total. I bought $1000 worth of books and telescopes, whatever I could buy, boxed them up and posted them. I took the *Reptiles in Colour* book my pop gave me and put it in the first box. I've never looked back.

What DeadlyScience gave me, which I didn't anticipate, was purpose. At first, my purpose was to work with animals and be a zookeeper. My purpose now is much greater. And I understand that what people thought I was capable of was a drastic underestimation. I did hack a government system when I was fifteen. You have to be pretty intelligent to do that. That my teachers failed to see it is a reflection on them, not me.

After I won the NSW Young Australian of the Year Award, I was in Dapto, walking through the mall, and I saw an old teacher. She said, 'Have you been working?' We were next to the newsagent, so I bought a copy of the *Illawarra Mercury*. I'm like, 'Here you go, have this.' The headline was, 'The 2020 NSW Young Australian of the Year is indigenous mentor and fundraiser Corey Tutt'. She contacted me later and said, 'Look, I'm really sorry for my comments, but I thought you were one of those students who was just going to be a derelict.' You know what? She was wrong. And you shouldn't say things like that, because you don't know what kids can do, and where they'll end up. One day they might be your boss.

I offered to speak to the students at my old school and ended up doing that. Thanks to my pop, I just roll with the punches. Ninety per cent of the attention I get is positive, but there's negative stuff too. Sometimes from our own people, sometimes from trolls. People say, 'Oh, you're not even that black,' or, 'You're white.' I block and move on. If I get upset, my partner says, 'They only care because they're not there.'

I've worked with kids in the jail system, kids who lost their homes during the bushfires, kids who had COVID-19 in Melbourne in the social housing towers. I've worked with kids who'd lost their parents, with a young girl whose mum had suicided. I taught a young fella who'd lost four siblings to suicide how to read, and he doesn't want to be a deadly footballer anymore; he wants to be a deadly geologist.

I spend my todays making tomorrows better. It's my mission. I've been in Redfern at 11 o'clock at night, trying to get kids to go home; I want them to have jobs and a future, not be on the wrong side of the law or dead. Mothers, fathers, kids write to me saying thank you for saving their son's life, their daughter's life. Sometimes it feels selfish, because I have a partner who loves me very much, but I would rather be on the phone with a kid who's about to kill themselves and talk them out of it.

DeadlyScience is online but not for marketing purposes. When you see a DeadlyScience post, you see hope, you see promise, you see Indigenous kids reading and doing science. Everyone needs to see this, particularly the kids. They need to know their people are proud of them.

When I was younger, I thought I probably *would* die young, by my own hand or my own fault, just like that career advisor told me. It's hard to explain these things. How to explain to your fiancée, who's not Indigenous, that your mum is a victim of childhood trauma? How to explain to your mother-in-law that your grandfather wasn't your dad's dad after all, but your mum's dad? How do you explain intergenerational trauma?

It's hard to talk about, but it needs to be told, because people don't understand. Sometimes I'm on TV, or in a newspaper article, and people say, 'Oh, you're so well spoken, you must be privately schooled.' And it's like, you have *no idea* what I've been through to get here.

But it's *because* of all I've gone through that I'm here. I never dreamed I'd teach kids how to read, that I'd write a book, that I'd be someone people looked up to. I've become a good person, an empathetic person, someone who matters *because* of the trauma. If I'd had respectable parents who invested in me, I don't know where I'd be. A mechanic, maybe. I'm handy. But I wouldn't care so much. I wouldn't be fighting to get books to kids. Fighting to get equal education. Fighting to give them identity and purpose. As an Indigenous man, as an emerging elder, I give back to the next generation. That is my role. I'm not there yet, but I *am* emerging.

PAUL
CAPSIS

It's been noted that reviews of Australia's premier cabaret artiste Paul Capsis read like religious awakenings. Ironic since he gave Catholicism the flick umpteen years ago, but such is his onstage power and wounded charisma that admirers reach for 'transcendent', 'transformative' and 'voice of an angel', before slowing to a halt and gazing off transfixed into the middle distance.

A universe away from the traditional Aussie archetype, Paul has made his mark on stages worldwide, from Vienna to Hong Kong, in plays and operas, and opposite Alex Dimitriades in the film *Head On*.

On the one hand, he's considered globe-straddling artistic director Barrie Kosky's muse; on the other, he's acclaimed for his striking, award-winning solo shows. Paul's cabarets showcase his supremely versatile singing voice, and ability to channel damaged divas from Billie Holiday to Janis Joplin. His one-man play *Angela's Kitchen*, in which he played multiple members of his family, is a tribute to his grandmother.

As a slight, sunny, softly spoken Maltese–Greek Australian boy growing up in Sydney with his grandmother in the 1970s, Paul experienced bullying so severe that it hindered his learning. If being gay is problematic now, back then it was an invitation for savage mistreatment, from teachers as well as students. Being a 'wog' didn't exactly help either.

Paul credits music with saving him during school, but with the benefit of hindsight, credits school for shaping him into the potent, determined, unique talent he is today. He was named the 2021 Adelaide Cabaret Festival Icon Award winner.

There was no bullying in the first three years. I went to a Catholic school and I was in love with the nuns. I thought the world was wonderful, people were nice, and everyone was free to sing and dance like the Elvis movies I watched on TV. But then Mum couldn't afford to send me there anymore, and when I was eight I went to a public school in the same suburb, Surry Hills, and it was *rough*, with a huge mix of cultures – Lebanese, Turkish, Aboriginal, everything.

From when I arrived there were comments: 'You sound like my sister,' 'You sound like my mother,' 'You're a girl, you're not really a boy.' But it was a magical time. I had a wonderful teacher who'd play Beatles records and wanted us to dance and sing and perform. Because of my Greek heritage, when we'd go to parties there'd be Turkish music and belly dancing, and this teacher, my favourite, encouraged me to belly dance in front of the school at assembly.

That was ... a huge mistake. She put on a track with sitar music from the *Sgt. Pepper's* album, and I got up, on my own, in my school uniform – in my *greys* – and did this dancing. It was hideous. *Terrible.* Everything changed; I was picked on every day. It was so full on.

And it went on, and on, and on. From teachers, too. I had a racist teacher in Grade 6 who picked on my brother and me because we were 'non-Australian'. So there was the wog thing, and the girly thing. I was eight when I first heard the word 'poofter'. I didn't know what it was, but I knew it was bad, because people *hated* me for it. A Greek boy said to me once, 'If I was like you, I would want my father to kill me. You're a disgrace to the Greeks.'

There were these brothers who used to wait for me after school finished, to hit and kick me. Sometimes just one little hit, one little kick and then walk away. They bashed my brother Manuel too, once. Not because he was a poofter. Because he had *asthma*. They saw us coming, basically. My father didn't raise us, so we didn't have that male thing, what to do in a fight. I had no idea. We weren't brought up with any guidance about how to protect yourself in a physical way.

Manuel's eighteen months older than me, and they made his nose bleed. I became hysterical, and screamed and shouted, and they freaked and stopped hitting him. This lying-in-wait thing went on for a while, but one day I'd had enough and defended myself. I went crazy, I laid into this boy, and a woman ran across the road and told me off. She called me a bully, and shouted at me to leave him alone. I'd begun developing this behaviour where I'd take it, take it, take it, and then I'd explode. They were clever enough not to hit or kick me where they could be caught, but when I retaliated, full of fury, it would be in front of the teacher and I'd get punished.

There was a Portuguese boy who would, every day, just slap me in the face. One day I picked him up, grabbed him by the collar and threw him so hard he went flying into chairs and tables, and then I burst into tears. We both got the cane.

I'd go into my mum's room and look in her dressing-table mirror, and stare at myself, for ages. I thought, 'There's something there that everyone sees but I don't. And if I look in the mirror I'll find it.' If I could find it, I thought, I could *change* it.

My grandmother raised me and Manuel. Mum lived nearby, more an older sister-type figure; someone I'd see every day, but she was there and gone. Discipline and leave. She was a black sheep, because of having two children and no husband. In her family, that was *big*. Dad was supposed to pay, but for whatever reason we wore hand-me-downs, Smith Family clothes. Our clothes were mismatched and odd, and I wore jackets from different schools.

So, pretty much, I was threatened a lot. And then, because I was still eleven at the end of Grade 6, they made me repeat a year. There were about nine of us who were the wrong age for high school. With the news that I had to stay there, with that horrible teacher, at that dreadful school, I told my grandmother I wasn't going back.

I'd heard about this other school, about five blocks away, and I went there by myself to meet the teachers, to find out if I could go there. I was in the Surry Hills area so they said yes. My mother said, 'No! You're not going there. You're not walking that far to school.' But my grandmother said to let me.

I had the best six months of my school life there. It was the polar opposite of the other place. The teachers were friendly and nice. The kids were nice. Everyone sang, everyone performed, everyone got on. I couldn't believe this place existed. I remember thinking, 'Why didn't I come here before?' I was absolutely devastated on my last day. I hid under the stairs and sobbed.

My brother was already at the high school I was going to, and he'd told me, 'All those boys are waiting for you. They told me, they're going to get you.' And I went to this school and it was everything my brother said. But worse.

It was a jail, built by convicts, and part of it still was a jail. The whole vibe of the school was jail. The teachers were like wardens, and the boys were out of control. The first thing I remember seeing was the woodwork teacher being chased by a class of boys across the grounds. I thought, 'If they can do that to a teacher, I'm f**ked.' And I was. It was ridiculous.

Nothing happened for six months, so I thought it was just a threat, but then it started, and it was every day. It was a nightmare. Even the teachers, especially the sports teachers. I'd go along to sports and do everything, but each time I was violently abused, and it just escalated. By Year 9 it was absolutely out of control. Even the headmaster was mortified by me.

In all the six years I spent there, I could not go into the playground. If I did I'd get water thrown on me, or kicked. I was called 'poofter' or 'faggot' every day. I was spat on. Clothes ripped. Punched. Hair pulled. By Year 9 I could only go to the toilet during class, when no one was around. But there was the odd kid who *would* be around. And they'd get me. This Turkish boy just came up once and punched me in the face. Said nothing. Just punched me and walked off.

I couldn't learn because I was anxious the whole time. I just couldn't learn. Every day was about how to get through the day. How do I survive until I get home? It was terrifying. My fantasy was, 'How can I become invisible?' Because there were boys who *were* kind of invisible. They didn't pull any attention at all. I dreamed of that. I tried once, cutting my hair really short like the others, and dressing like them, but I still had my voice and I was still *me*. It didn't work. It was still the same. So I went, 'Oh well, f**k it.'

I didn't have strategies, apart from *not* being out in the playground. I knew I couldn't be outside. But there were teachers that were very good to me, and it helped. Over the years, as the violence got worse, some of them – my art, music and English teachers – went to great lengths to help protect me. They'd lock me in the art room during recess. But of course, sometimes you'd go to class and the teacher wasn't there yet. It might only be five minutes, but that's all they needed to get me.

The worst day of my life was in Year 9. I was in art class and the teacher was late – it was funny, because she was one who protected me – but a boy hit me, or said something, and I picked up this broom handle and whacked him with it. That's when the teacher walked in, and I got in trouble. She threw me out of the class. I lost it. I smashed the window. I wanted to jump. We were on the third floor. I would've died, and I wanted to. Being hated by so many people at once, all the time; it does your head in. I got cut. There was blood and glass everywhere. I was a mess, an absolute mess. The teacher was so, so sorry. I was standing there sobbing, covered in blood. They left me alone for a little while after that. They went, 'He's nuts.'

Year 9 was intense. Pretty severe. I got bashed by another group of older, football-playing boys. I was doing my usual avoiding thing, going through the corridors when no one else was around, and I ran into these boys who'd just come out of class. They bashed and kicked me in the corridor. I had my first out-of-body experience. My body left me and I observed what was happening – and I felt *nothing*. I was completely numb.

I threw my schoolbag, I ran out of the school. I didn't look; I was just running. It was on a busy street, this school; I could have been killed. My mother went and saw the principal, and because I knew some of those boys' names, they got badly punished. They got like nine whips of the cane, and didn't touch me again.

I wanted to leave, but my English teacher told my mother not to let me. He said, 'You'll have this problem wherever he goes. It will disrupt his education, and the other boys are starting to mature.' So I stayed. I was the first one in my family to ever do Year 12. Not one single member of my family had done their HSC before. My brother had left. He hated it, he couldn't cope, and after Year 9 he was gone.

I was determined, because I didn't want to be a cleaner. I didn't want to do those physical, menial jobs like my family. After Year 10 my grandmother said to me, 'Y'know you've probably had enough school now. Get out of there now.' And I said, 'No, it's better now,' and I stayed. Which I found bizarre even to myself.

Things *had* changed by Year 10. It was a bit better. A lot of the violent boys left after Year 9; my real problems, the real bad cases, they went out into the workforce. There was a different energy; I was older, and by then I had developed a very tough sort of persona. I got a reputation; if you hassled me, you'd get the tongue. You'd get a piece.

I'd developed the comeback and I'd stand my ground and give it to them. Unsparingly. I wanted them to feel what I felt. I'd attack them: their physicality, their family – I'd go all out. I publicly took on the gay thing, and had some fun with it. If someone hassled me I'd say, 'Yeah, I *am* gay, but I wouldn't suck *your* cock. That tiny thing!' They'd be, 'You're mad!' I was incredibly defiant, even though I hadn't had sex, I hadn't done anything with anyone.

I really rebelled, and music was a *massive*, massive factor. It saved me. I would go home after school, turn off the lights, and lie in my bedroom and listen to Janis Joplin. There was something in her voice that helped me, that gave me strength. The way she sang, the way she *screamed*, something in her voice was like an angel with big wings. She helped me from the grave.

Janis was my hero, my role model. I read about her, and she was bullied. At university they voted her 'ugliest man on campus', and we're talking Texas in the late '50s. And the more stuff they did, the more defiant and the tougher she became. She was so defiant. As my obsession with her escalated, that's when I became very 'Janis' tough. Yeah. I'm gonna wear a vest, and my hair long, f**k you.

She was my armour. In all the quotes I read she said, 'I'm gonna be myself, I don't give a shit. I'm *me.* I don't care!' That's what I grabbed onto. I thought, 'Well, they're telling me I'm different too. They all hate me too. But look at her, she's a *rock star*.' She was powerful. And that's kind of what inspired me to perform, as well. I was into any women singers who were tough. That's what I liked. Because my grandmother was very strong and tough, and my mother too. They're 'no shit' women.

I remember praying a lot when I was a child. Praying for people to stop hitting me. Praying really hard. So by seventeen, I was like, this religion thing is *bullshit.* I'm gay, and I wanna have nothing to do with this hateful thing that tries to make me scared, with its heaven and hell and good and bad. *Hateful.*

Coming to terms with being gay was very difficult. When I was seventeen, and realised I *was* gay, I didn't accept it. I had a lot of self-hatred going on. I was very depressed, suicidal, because I thought life was bleak. I was gay and hated. I'd try saying to myself, 'No, no. You're not. Really, you're not.' But I was. And I didn't want to be gay. I hated it. Other kids have fun in high school, sexually experimenting. Not me. Being 'gay' brought so much misery, the last thing I wanted to do was engage in it. I was terrified and confused. Part of me thinks, 'Oh, I wish I'd had some fun,' but it wasn't safe for me.

A couple of times I was violently approached at school by older boys, one of them pushing me to the floor of a toilet cubicle and screaming, 'Suck my cock!' He had his pants down and was frothing at the mouth. There was a bit of that. But there were also these wonderful teachers who would talk to me, and say, 'It's okay if you are gay.'

I was very late in learning because of all the anxiety, but in Years 10, 11 and 12, because I could finally relax, my brain started taking in information, and I was coming first in things like art, ancient history and geography. And I had teachers I looked up to, who I loved, and who loved me. I think I made it because I developed some fight and because there was support. There were a few kind people around, and sometimes that's all you need.

I'm glad I stayed on till Year 12. Because it did shift, it did change. And that's why I'm talking about this now, because I've been hearing a lot about bullying and suicides. But even without suicide, it's about how bullying scars you. And you've got to deal with that shit. You can't have that experience and then expect for it not to impact. I look back now and realise, *of course* enduring abuse like that has some kind of long-term effect.

When I left high school I was very, very, *very* f**king angry. For *years* I was so angry. Then, through my twenties, I went through a time of forgiveness. I thought about it a lot, tried to figure out *why* they were so cruel, and I felt sad for those boys. Like, what were *they* going through to do that to someone else? They were having shit in their own lives; I think their parents were violent.

I had therapy, because I thought I'd dealt with it, but I hadn't. I had no self-confidence, no self-esteem. I was hated for so long, why would anyone want me? And I'd just come out and started having relationships, and then it was the AIDS crisis. I thought, 'Wow. I'm being *punished*.' I was too scared to do anything with anyone. In my late twenties I started having panic attacks, and they were pretty severe. A couple of times I took myself to hospital, because I thought I was dying. So I had to do something. I started meditation, I read self-help books, and I began therapy.

But my life started after I finished high school. It's like I was born then. Everything changed. In the years after school, gradually people became my friends, and they thought I was funny, and they liked me. And I had one friend from primary school, Mark, a tall Anglo guy, and he stayed my friend right through high school even though it meant he copped it too. He's the one who got me into community theatre when I left school. I joined Shopfront Theatre, and the five years I spent there was the first experience, other than the six months at that school I found for myself, where I thought maybe the world was okay.

I'm very grateful to the theatre, because it educated me. It made up for years of not being able to learn, because I was in a world where I had to absorb information, and research, and learn scripts. I also credit my grandmother's upbringing, because she was a fiercely determined woman. She had no education. She told me, 'You have to go to school or you'll be like me, not able to read or write.' But she worked three jobs and she had six kids. I felt safe with her, and she raised me to *work*.

To be really honest, because I made it that way, school became a positive learning experience for me. It made me wary and distrustful of people, but it toughened me, gave me a more realistic view of what humanity is about. I have a very, very low tolerance for bad behaviour or disloyalty. If people cross me, betray me, backstab me, dishonour me or whatever, it's *over*. Anything dodgy in relationships, I leave. We're not here for long, and I want to surround myself with beautiful people. And you can make that choice.

There was a lesson in it. It gave me a real sense of survival, of not giving up; I wasn't going to allow people to stop me. That's come in useful. Everybody said to me that I'd never make it as a performer. Because I'm a wog. Because I'm a poofter. Because I'm girly. The list went on. You're short. You're big nosed. Everything. I got it all. But I persisted. Because I'm incredibly stubborn and determined. I thought, 'Y'know what? If it's true I don't accept it. I'm gonna do it anyway.'

It's shaped me. Everything I've done as a performer has gone a long way from what I was supposed to be. I started creating my own cabaret work in my twenties, and that's what I'm now known for. Because I was like, 'Yeah, I'm just gonna be me. I've got to create my own work.' Every artist I admire didn't follow a pattern; they were groundbreakers. And now I see people copying me, doing bits of my stuff; I see that coming up now, which is fabulous. And I've had lots of young people over the years write to me – girls, boys, gay, straight, wog, Anglo. They relate.

I don't need people's blessing like I used to. I don't have that incredible need to be liked. I accept that I will be unliked, and liked. That's the world. And I like my life now. I've had some difficult things to deal with, but it's never stopped me from being who I am.

I distinctly remember thinking, after wanting to kill myself, that I was going to do the opposite. *Because* I'm so hated, I'm going to do everything in my power to have a good life and not self-destruct. I'm not going to do to myself what's been done to me. That's why I haven't done drugs. I was clear minded about wanting to be an artist, and I wasn't going to let addiction get in the way. I'm surprised at how determined and adamant about choices I've been.

I'm so glad now that I didn't self-harm, that I didn't kill myself. Oh my god. I would have missed out on a lot of fabulous life. A lot of incredible experiences. I'm very grateful I've had them, as an artist and as a person.

I'm becoming more powerful as I get older, and I hardly think about those times now. I'm not the same person I was five years ago, ten years ago. For sure. I'd have loved to have been like I am now in my twenties, or in school. It would have been very different. But what's the point of saying that? Because all that had to happen for me to get to here.

PENNY
WONG

Politics isn't easy. The hours are gruelling, everyone hates you, and you're constantly being baited, bitched about, trolled and stabbed in the back. No matter your views on Penny Wong's politics, it's impossible to not be impressed by her grace under pressure. First as Finance Minister and later as Leader of the Opposition in the senate, Penny is the cool, calm and collected eye in the storm of federal government.

Penny's bulletproof and calm demeanour is essential in a frequently hostile work environment. In the homogenous sea of – still – mostly middle-aged white guys, she's not only a woman, but the first Asian-born Federal Senator, and the first female member of a federal cabinet to be openly LGBTQIA+. She is also a practising Christian, and was instrumental in legalising same-sex marriage.

Penny started honing her 'sticks and stones' armoury at primary school. Born in Malaysia, Penny moved to the Adelaide Hills when her parents broke up, and her Australian mum, Jane, returned home. Penny and younger brother, Toby, were the first Asians that anyone in 1970s suburban Adelaide had clapped eyes on, and they were seen as an exotic sideshow. Or worse.

Penny pretended not to care, studied assiduously to compensate, and developed a hard-won understanding of discrimination. Her path became even more challenging when Toby took his own life in 2002. Penny, who found her way to politics through law, and now as a mother, remains determined to battle prejudice and change people's attitudes for the better.

Primary school was a real shock to the system. I had bad migraines for a couple of years, and my mum took me to the doctors to check my eyes and stuff, because they were so bad I'd get double vision. I've never had anything like it since, and I suspect it was the stress of moving to Adelaide, not living with my father any more, leaving the home and culture I knew, and coming to this cold place where people had a go at me.

School was, I'd have to say, a pretty difficult time in my life and in my family's lives. I don't want to overstate it, because we had parents who loved us, and food on the table, and there are many kids who have a harder life than that. But we did cop a fair bit about our race at school, and from one of the neighbours who just – she just had a problem. It varied from people who asked questions because we were new and different, to people who were obviously prejudiced.

I came to Australia in 1977, when I was eight, and we lived in the Adelaide Hills. The community wasn't very culturally diverse, and my brother and I were the first Asians that I know of. We were certainly the first people of Asian background to go to that school.

The school I went to in Malaysia was completely different. It was diverse, very multicultural. It was an international school, and had kids from every background you could imagine; there were lots of British, Australian and Canadian expats, and kids from the local community whose parents wanted an English-based education, so lots of Indians, Chinese and Malay.

When we went to get enrolled at school in Adelaide, my mum and I walked across the asphalt, through the schoolyard, and the children literally formed a path around us and on either side, and commented on me. They were saying, 'What is she?', and someone said, 'She's Hong Kong-ese,' and I'm thinking, 'There's no such thing, what are they talking about?' I realised for the first time that my race was something that people would notice, that it was an issue.

It was all about race. My sexuality wasn't an issue at school, because it wasn't formative. It was much later in my life that I entered a relationship with a woman. I get it a bit now, though!

I never like to talk about some of the things I remember. I'm not sure if it's because it brings back how it felt to hear it, or whether it's because I don't like to repeat words of hate. It's hard to talk about, and it's very hard to talk about my brother. I think he probably had fewer defences than I did. People are born differently, and I suppose he was more vulnerable and gentle, which is a beautiful thing, but it's harder in the world.

I dealt with it by trying not to respond. I tried to ignore it, and not show if it hurt. It was, 'I'm never going to let you see, in any way, that this gets to me. I'm never going to let you see that I feel upset, or lonely, or shy.'

And I also did it by trying to be better than the people who were teasing me, so I have no doubt I became much more focused on studying, getting good marks, doing well on the sporting field, those sorts of things. I decided I was going to be better than them, and achieve in this field, and this field, and this field.

I was trying to prove that I could succeed no matter what they said to me, and no matter what they thought of me. That I could do well no matter what they threw at me. It wasn't so much to get people to like me, to become my friend; it was that I wasn't going to allow them to keep me down. My reaction was to want to get better marks in the test, or do well in the relay or pool.

I didn't become insular. I've seen that happen with kids, but that wasn't my response. I just pretended to be confident, even when I wasn't. I learned to be steady and still, even when it felt very messy and difficult. You know, to hold yourself steady, even if your reactions are really strong and your emotions confused.

It wasn't easy. It got better as time went on. I learned a lot. I learned how to rise above things, or at least pretend that I was. I also found that for most people – not all, but for *most* people – prejudice doesn't survive personal relationship. Sometimes it would come out in different ways: 'We don't like Asians, but you're okay,' which I always thought was kind of funny. But sometimes children say things and you can't blame them, because they're just repeating what they hear around the table at home.

My mum was a lot of support. She would come up with one-liners of varying degrees of utility. I think she found it very hard to have her children targeted, and to be essentially powerless to stop it. Like all you can do is love them and support them, and try and help them with strategies to handle it, but ultimately they've got to go out and handle it themselves. That was very hard for her.

And look, I was lucky. Mum's from a family of five girls, and my aunts were really good, particularly Ally. She was great, incredibly loving and incredibly supportive, and the attitude was, 'Don't let them get to you, they're not worth it.' So I drew a lot of strength from my family.

I suppose in hindsight, I have learned a lot from school. It taught me you have to try and turn the things that life throws at you to good. You know, use negative experiences, and make the best of them, because sometimes you can learn from them in ways that do help you later.

I found high school a lot easier than primary school. When I went to Scotch College, I found there was a lot less racism. The teachers there were more supportive, and there were more things I could do, so I was able to engage more.

But, you know, because of my experiences at school, I know what it's like to be different, and to be targeted because of it, and it probably influenced my decision to go into politics. I'm sure you can trace that desire in me to change things for the better to my childhood. If I hadn't gone into politics I would have done something else consistent with those beliefs.

Interestingly, I've certainly not lived a life where I've avoided monocultures. In fact, if you look at the choices I've made around career, I've put myself into environments that were not particularly diverse at all, you know, whether it was the trade union movement or legal work or Parliament.

When I entered Parliament, there was me, Senator Tsebin Tchen from Victoria, and at that stage Michael Johnson may or may not have been in the Parliament – his mother was from Hong Kong – and there was the woman who worked in the library. In this huge building, that was it, apart from, you know, the cleaners. There are Greek and Italian MPs today, from the more settled communities, but we still don't have a Parliament that's as diverse as the Australian community.

I have no doubt it's easier for me to navigate through that environment because of my school experience, because the hardest part of it is how you think about it internally, how you manage it inside you. I know I started to learn how to do that at school. In the end, politics isn't that different from the schoolyard.

I absolutely learned pretty early on how things that are wrong can become accepted, and how important it is to stand against them. I still react when there are issues of race, where I think the other side are toying with the sorts of prejudices we know do exist. I do react, and there is a personal basis to that.

For people like me, racial discrimination is not an abstract principle, it's about our lives. And I haven't lived the hardest life – I'm a senator and it's an extraordinary and privileged life in many ways – but when you talk about prejudice or discrimination to someone like me, it's different than to someone who's had no experience of it.

It's much less now – I think Australia's a very different place from what it was like in the 1970s and early '80s. But on occasion, someone will still abuse me in the street, or something else, and whenever I've told my friends, they're surprised it happens.

I once read a comment by an Aboriginal woman – I can't recall who it was – where she talked about the concept of parallel universes here in Australia. She said, 'The Australia I live in is not the one you live in; when I walk along the street, or when I go somewhere, how I'm seen and how I'm treated, is a different world to yours.'

I remember thinking, 'I understand some part of that.' Not *as* much, because I think Aboriginal Australians have had the most sustained level of discrimination of any group in our society. But my experience of what it was like to be in this country was very different even from people who were close to me. Because they just couldn't comprehend that people would be like that, whereas I knew they could.

It's so important for political leaders and politicians to stand up on issues of prejudice, even if they're not personally affected, because it's about the sorts of values and ethics you're backing in the community. It's the easiest thing in the world to speak to people's fears, and it's the wrong thing to do. The positions we hold shouldn't be used like that.

I try and bring the values I have, and the ethics in which I believe, to the job. They include a view about equality, and I was part of the pushing for the affirmative action changes inside the party. I think that people can be better, less willing to turn on others, more open-hearted and more open-minded. That's a belief I've brought to my political life.

Part of why I've always been completely open about my relationship [with Sophie Allouache], if not interested in having a long discussion about the detail of it, is I just thought it was important to normalise it publicly. To say, 'This neither makes me less, nor more, qualified to do what I'm doing.' Being open about it was a statement in itself, I think. Normalising being different is important, because being different is okay.

I thought it was really interesting, the difference between my first swearing-in and the second. For the first swearing-in they photographed Sophie and mum and it gets on the front page of the papers and people comment about it, right? The first time a same-sex partner goes to a ministerial swearing-in! The second time, not even commented on, not even a photo. I thought that was fantastic, like that's a really good indication of a step being taken.

I think, 'What do we aspire to?' One of the things I aspire to is a nation in which we genuinely are judged – and succeed or not – on the basis of our abilities and our character, and not on our attributes. Not on where we were born, or where we went to school, or how wealthy our parents are, or whether we're gay or straight or white or not. That's where we should always be walking towards.

BRENDAN
COWELL

Brendan Cowell is remarkable. Sure, he's an award-winning novelist, actor and scriptwriter, but more impressive is that at school he was good at sport and still deeply unpopular. In Australia, that takes talent.

Born and bred in Cronulla, NSW, and living with three women from the age of thirteen, Brendan was a poor fit at his all-boys school from the start, foisting personal poetry and flamboyant dance routines on his resistant schoolmates. Unsurprisingly, he was considered a weirdo and viewed with suspicion and hostility.

Things escalated when he started appearing on telly. A high profile is a mixed blessing at any school. Despite being depressed, and routinely ostracised and taunted, Brendan didn't change his behaviour one iota and kept reading his poetry out at assembly and putting on peculiar shows.

In the end it paid off. By the time he graduated he'd gone from being the freak to one of the cool guys, and kids came to see his plays instead of calling him names from a distance. This insistence on staying true to himself has translated into a rich, prolific and satisfying career.

Brendan has written eleven plays, including *Bed*, which won the Patrick White Playwright's Award. He starred in the Foxtel series *Love My Way*, *Howzat! Kerry Packer's War*, the film *Noise*, and wrote for *Love My Way* and *The Slap*. He also wrote and starred in the feature film *Save Your Legs*. His first novel, *How It Feels*, is a dark coming-of-age novel based on his experiences and observations growing up in Cronulla, his second, *Plum*, is another dive into Australian men in crisis.

I was a weirdo. Everyone just thought I was a bit of a weirdo. At primary school I was into cricket and rugby league, basketball and stuff, but when I'd invite boys from school over, I'd want to choreograph a dance routine to 'The Power of Love' by Huey Lewis and the News, and they'd just want to go fishing or terrorise something. I was always wanting to make little plays, and entertain and stuff, and they'd be like, 'Why do you want to do a f**king dance routine for?' I think I freaked everybody out.

A couple of the guys stopped asking me over as much, and I was skateboarding with a gang, and all of a sudden I didn't know where they were skateboarding. A few guys didn't want to come over anymore because I wanted to dance with them. They probably thought it was a bit gay or something.

But ever since I can remember, on Friday nights, I got my nan and my mum and we'd have Red Faces like that thing on *Hey Hey It's Saturday*. I was four or five, and I was all the contestants on Red Faces – I'd have five things prepared – and they had to pick a winner. I'd have, like, a Michael Jackson impersonation, then a poem I'd written called something like 'Staring at Puddles'. Then I'd sing 'Shaddup Your

Face', and, um, tell them a story, and impersonate someone from my school. I mean, seriously, what was I doing? But I've always been, 'Hey, you gotta watch this!' I just wanted to get in front of people.

I got into telly by accident. I spent a lot of time in my youth, with my mum, waiting outside dance studios and ballet halls for my sisters. We were in this waiting room one time, and there were like twenty kids who looked like me, blue eyes and chubby cheeks, and one by one they were going off into this room. And then a guy came out and said, 'Right, okay, you're next', and I was like, 'What?' But I went in, and ate some cornflakes, and said, 'Yum', and the guy went, 'You've got a good head, kid, who's your agent?' And I said, 'What's an agent?' So he hooked me up with an agent, I got the cornflakes ad, and I was away. Eating and smiling on television.

So I was in and out with friends at primary school, but it wasn't too bad. But as soon as I turned ten, till I was about fifteen, it was really hard. From when I was on the telly a bit, that's when the bad times started. It was a very lonely few years; I had no friends and it was pretty depressing. The guys at school figured that if you're on telly you think you're better than everyone. I didn't think that. I was just making money, having fun, and it made me feel good. I definitely didn't flaunt it.

But then I'd go to school and everyone'd make a big deal of it, make fun of me, and terrorise me. I had some scary walks home, with kids I knew forming circles around me, yelling and calling me names.

I was doing TV ads, for Pavlova Magic, and Crisco Oil, and My Juice is Fruity, and kids would form a circle around me, and sing the ad, and push me around. Other kids would call me 'moo cow'.

About 30 of them would get around me and moo at me, like cows, all the way to getting my bike. It sounds silly, but at the time it's really scary.

I remember turning down a couple of things, because I just kept thinking, 'If I do that, what will they sing? What will happen?' Particularly when I got the Combantrin commercial. I would have had to say, 'I've got worms,' and I thought, 'I can't do that.' Can you imagine? 'I've got worms,' and then going to school the next day? I would have been crucified. So I turned it down for my own protection, even though it was like $5000.

For a long time I was really sad, really alone. Just riding my bike home on my own, and walking back through the bush on my own, and day after day seeing everyone hanging out having icy poles, riding their boards, and me thinking, 'Nobody wants to hang out with me. Like no one. Everybody hates me.'

I really couldn't make a friend; I kept trying. I had one friend in kindergarten who was Vietnamese, and he was my best friend for four years, but his family were refugees who had come over by boat and the government deemed them to be illegally here so they got deported back to Vietnam when he was in Year 6. And he was it until Year 9. It gets to you. I mean, it's the weekend, and everyone else is over at their mate's house, and being invited to parties, and you're just hanging with your mother. On a Saturday!

I had some really dark thoughts. I thought all sorts of things. I thought I was a freak, and I thought about running away, and I thought about dying. I thought I was a pain to everyone. It was awful. I know my mother was incredibly worried about me. She was getting me to read books, get into theatre, and trying to fill my head with ideas of another land, another place, a life out of the Shire and out of the school.

I was starting to be on TV more and more. I was hosting an afternoon show with Cameron Daddo, and doing breakfast TV and I was on *A Country Practice* or *Sons and Daughters* and you know, I was on telly a fair bit.

I started to have a bit of a voice at school and it wasn't exactly welcomed. I was writing poetry and reading it at assembly, and doing weird performance stuff, which is not gonna help your cause. Not in Cronulla. I created a suggestion box in the library and at assembly. I said, um, 'I want to know all the suggestions of things that students want at the school; we can put money in for charities, we can have entertainment nights or talent quests.' I said that I'd pool the suggestions, and approach the staff and see if we could get some fundraising for things that the students want in the school.

And everyone just wrote, 'I suggest Brendan Cowell should just get f**ked', 'I suggest we should have a surfing competition and Brendan Cowell should get f**ked', and, ah, 'I think Brendan Cowell is gay, and I suggest you go and suck a dick.' They weren't exactly, you know, what I was hoping for.

One day this guy, who was the captain of the rugby union team, got this rumour going that he was going to fight me on the oval at 3.30pm. I didn't even know him, and the whole school was going, 'You're going to fight this guy,' and I thought he was going to kill me. Now, this is a pretty wimpy thing to do, but I went to the principal's office, and I said, 'Hey, um, this guy wants to fight me today, and I don't really know him and I don't want to fight him.' And the principal of the school looked at me and said, 'Well, there's certain things a man has to do to be respected by his peers,' and he just walked off. I mean, what?!

So I rolled up. I went, 'Hey man, I don't want to fight you,' and he came up and smacked me in the head twice. I fell over and said, 'You win, man', shook his hand, got on my bike and rode off. Weirdly, a lot of people respected me after that.

After my parents divorced at thirteen, I spent most of my time with mum and my two sisters, and my nan, and they were all strong, opinionated, kinda alpha women, so I didn't have problems talking with women. Our school took girls in from Year 10, and the guys started looking at me going, 'Holy shit, Brendan Cowell is talking to the girls.' I was just talking to them; I didn't have a lot of action, but I had a lot of female company.

I was pretty charming with the ladies early on, you know? I was vice captain of my school (due to the fact only a couple of us put our names in for election), and I'd do debating, we'd have meetings with other schools, and all the girls who were valedictorians and school captains really liked me. 'Cause I was cheeky and smart and I wasn't like all the other dopey guys at school who just sneered at girls or worse.

It all changed when I met Johnny, this Scottish guy, who had pimples all over his face, and had just arrived in the country. We instantly became friends. And then there was Bart, a big six-foot-four guy who kinda looked after me a lot. Then suddenly our good looks started forming, Johnny's pimples went away, we formed a band and it just made everything cool and better.

We started going to rave parties and wearing baggy pants and stripey shirts, and all of a sudden everyone wanted to know what we were doing. They heard we were going to nightclubs and hanging out with girls, and taking our parents' cars out, and all of a sudden everyone was like, 'Holy shit, these are the coolest guys in the school.' And we were! All of a sudden we were very popular. We had an air of mystique about us, we became a bit dangerous and a bit cool and a bit revered.

By Year 11 I was dating the hottest girl in Year 11, I was putting plays on and people were coming to see them, and I'd get up and speak at assembly and they'd applaud me, you know. So I went from being the kid that got laughed at, and mocked, and ostracised and all that shit to, 'That's that Cowell guy.' It turned right around for me.

I think it was because I never stopped being who I was, you know? I didn't go, 'Okay, I'll be like the rest of you.' I thought, 'F**k ya, I'm going to be me, and I'm going to take it, and take it, and take it, until you accept it.' Then they accepted it and they wanted to be a part of it.

And I kept being myself because I didn't know what else to do. My mum told me not to stop being myself, and I had this burning thing in me. I thought, 'Well, you've made me the weirdo, you've made me the outcast, and so I will be.'

I took a lot from that period. It's made me who I am. I think you gotta hang onto your voice, and you'll be rewarded. If your voice is pure it'll find its place eventually, as much as people try to drown it out, trample on it, and make it sound more like theirs and more like everybody else's.

Australians in general like affable people and harmless people and it was the same at school. Don't shine, don't be special, don't be irregular, and don't do anything that's not in line with everybody else. I didn't listen to that, so I got punished, and even now, I feel as an artist

I say too much about the problems in this country.

I just wrote a novel about youth suicide in Cronulla, because it's got the highest youth suicide rate in the country, and a lot of my friends took their own lives when I was at school. People from where I'm from really don't like that I've done it. But someone's got to say it, and – maybe it's from that time – I just went, 'F**k it, I'm going to be that guy.' I might be ostracised or unpopular, but it's a choice you make to put yourself in that part of society, and I think I made it early on.

It's hard to have perspective when you're young – you can't shoot out of your life and look at it. I reckon that's why a lot of kids take their lives. If a girl dumps you at school and everyone laughs at you, you don't know that you'll have twenty more girlfriends, then marry a beautiful woman that you'll meet on holiday in Bali in eight years' time, have three children, and be successful in what you do.

You just think, 'This is the end of the f**king world,' and that every feeling you're having right now are the only feelings you'll ever have, you'll never escape them, and that's the end. I had those thoughts but I somehow got through. But I had a mother and a father who kept telling me I had something to give, and one of those drama teachers who went, 'You've got to make waves, you've got something.' Even if they're the minority, a couple of those people can really change your life.

I'm grateful to all those guys that dumped me in the urinal, threw eggs at my head, 'mooed' me, called me names and chased me out of the school grounds. All of it. Yeah. I see them now, when I go to Cronulla, and they're fat and bending corrugated iron in the factory. And I don't think, 'F**k you, look who won.' I just think, 'You never grew.'

They never challenged themselves, never got out, never went through anything. They just picked on everyone that was different, and I was different, and they didn't stop me. And that's the important thing: find a way to not let people stop you being who you are.

TIFFINY
HALL

Tiffiny Hall, a 6th Dan Taekwondo black belt, Logie nominee, and celebrity trainer with her own fitness program, range of sportswear and supplements, surely sailed through high school with minions in her wake. Not so much. A stressed-out kid with braces, glasses, and cystic acne, Tiffiny was shy, socially anxious, and incapable of standing up for herself. She also preferred cleaning the house to hosting sleepovers. She was totes unpopular and essentially 6th Dan 'uncool'.

Literary by nature, Tiffiny was a closet creative in an ultra-sporty household that ran on Olympic-level discipline. Despite encouragement from her Year 6 English teacher, children's writer John Marsden, she swallowed her impractical ambition to be an author, and studied hard to prove she wasn't a 'dumb blonde'.

Tiff found fame on television as 'Angel' on *Gladiators*, as a coach on *The Biggest Loser*, and on *The Circle*, but she couldn't let writing go. She won the John Marsden Award for Creative Writing, and went on to fulfil her fiction writing dream.

Her debut novel was *White Ninja*, the first in her Roxy Ran martial arty children's fiction series, followed by *Red Samurai* and *Black Warrior*. Including health and fitness titles, she's got thirteen books under her (black) belt. Reinvented as the 'white ninja', Tiffiny is now the ambassador for her parents' Taekwondo schools, and besides delivering anti-bullying and self-esteem programs, she promotes the mindfulness benefits of Taekwondo.

As a one-time highly strung little misfit, she has a bottomless well of empathy for kids and adults with low self-worth, which drives her passion for coaching. And these days she's a lot pickier about friendships.

As a kid I was extremely shy; up until fourteen I'd say I was *paralysed* with shyness. I couldn't ask questions in class, and if we were at a restaurant I'd get my younger sister, Bridget, to order food for me. I hated conflict. It's bizarre really, because I was brought up with taekwondo, it's like oxygen to me, I'm a black belt, but I was shy at my core. I could do the moves, but I wasn't the fighter I should have been.

My love was creative writing. I always wanted to write, and in Year 5, when I was ten, John Marsden came to my school and became my English teacher. I was totally inspired and wanted to be an author more than anything, but I grew up in this really sporty household where I was being groomed to be an athlete. Being creative was considered 'fluffy', so I suppressed it. I shut that side down and didn't tell anybody. Strangely, my sister also shut down her creative side – she's a fashion designer now. My parents were extremely driven, both black belts. My dad was a fighter on the world circuit and an Olympic coach. He lives every day like he's a champion. Being in martial arts he's very focused on goals, on achieving the next rank, and that's what I grew up around.

So, writing was a bit of a dirty secret. I'd write in my bedroom on my own. I liked to write books and play piano, but whenever I was doing either I felt like I should be studying or training. My parents didn't say anything, but it felt like I wasn't being productive, like I wasn't achieving anything. I realise now, though, that I was getting *everything* out of it. It was how I dealt with stress; writing or playing was my time to be with myself. Doing creative writing felt 'naughty' because it didn't seem as disciplined as other, more serious, pursuits. But, as I've found out, it takes a lot of discipline to finish a book.

Like I said, I was very shy, and I always listened to what other people wanted from me. I didn't even pursue creative writing at uni, because my course advisor in Year 10 told me that if I wanted to be a writer, well, 'Would I like fries with that?' I was told I'd end up working at McDonalds. I ended up studying journalism for five years, and I hated every minute. I wasn't a huge victim of bullying at school, but I was a huge victim of 'self' bullying. I've always tried to be the best at everything and it's emotionally exhausting. There's no 'perfect'. You're always going to be disappointed. I really wanted that A-plus score at the end of Year 12; the highest you can get is 99.5. I got 98.75 and I was devastated.

I was a stressed-out kid. I stressed over everything, even things that should have been fun, like sports and swimming carnivals. I'd feel sick the night before. I was always a perfectionist, trying to do the right things in the right way. It started in Year 6 and just got worse and worse, the stress to achieve. To get those perfect straight A's. To not be the 'dumb blonde'.

I went to a very cliquey private girls' school and I never fitted in. There was a big fight in Year 6, and another in Year 9, all the girls just at each other, and I didn't know what to do. There was a lot of bullying going on between the different groups: it was verbally violent, and I hate conflict and couldn't deal with it. At a girls' school you have to choose sides – you know, hate *that* group and be loyal to *this* group – 'mean girls' stuff. But I was such a people-pleaser! I wanted to be liked, to participate, and do the right thing, I would never choose a side. So I wasn't very popular, and they decided I was a 'dumb blonde'.

After that I think I just carried the stereotype with me. Academically, I was no all-rounder; I was very strong in English – I couldn't spell that well but I always had a go, and I could express myself – but I struggled with maths and science. I needed a lot of help, and I dropped maths the first chance I got. I worked *really* hard to get good marks to subvert that dumb-blonde stereotype. I guess I still carry it somewhat as an adult, particularly with media and television. I'm not, actually, a 'stupid' presenter, or a 'dumb personal trainer'. People on social media are very keen to have a go at you, but I've learned to not take that on.

When I was fifteen, I was in the musical *42nd Street*, and it happened again. It was my first time on stage, and I could hardly dance and definitely couldn't sing, but I wanted to participate. The lead guy came from another school and was much older; he was eighteen, drove a car, and was the first guy most of us had seen. After the show finished he gave out awards to everyone, 'The girl most likely to go on and be a star,' stuff like that. He gave me an award for being 'The girl most likely to become a porn star.' I ... I couldn't breathe. I'd never even spoken to him. It was the most embarrassing moment of my life. It was terrible. Terrible. He kept calling me to go up on stage, and all the girls were laughing. That was it for me. I became utterly determined to get those perfect marks.

School stressed me out so much that I got glandular fever, which led to chronic fatigue syndrome, and I had to take six or seven months off. I think I was the first student in history ordered by teachers *not* to do homework, because I was studying so much. However, the reason I got sick was because I was trying to finish a novel late at night. I'd do my homework, and then around 10pm, I'd start writing well into the morning. I was obsessed with writing these books and, look, they're probably really bad, they'll never see the light of day, but I'd write one after the other, and put them in manilla folders under my bed.

That was Year 9, the pivotal time when you make your friends, and by the time I came back the friendship groups had been formed. People had paired off. Socially, I never recovered from that. I do regret making myself so busy. I always prioritised doing taekwondo, or sport, or playing the piano, or trumpet, all those things I did, over my friends. I'd do that instead of going to a sleepover. Now, later in life, I wish I'd placed more importance on those internal needs – my creativity, self-expression, and friendships.

Another disruption, I guess, was that mum became pregnant when I was sixteen. It was such a shock! My brother's the best thing now, he's a teenager and so funny, but a two-year-old getting into your things? When you're sixteen, seventeen, and wanting to be more independent, boys are coming on the scene, and you're trying to study? Bridget and I pitched in with babysitting, and that was my choice, I wanted to be around him, but, yeah, absolutely, no one else's mum was pregnant in Years 9 or 10.

I never fitted in. The school was multicultural, all the Italian girls stuck together, and a lot of the girls were really well off, and *they* stuck together. The dominant thing was wealth and having the 'right' things – it even went down to having a certain type of calculator. There was a lot of talk about money, having the right car, that sort of stuff. One girl was bullied because her family *rented* their BMW.

My mum would pick me up in the Tarago – a 'ninja' van that was sign-written with 'Get Your Kicks Here', and 'Fitness for Fun' down the side – wearing her white taekwondo uniform. It wasn't cool. It was a family business, and they'd take me and my sister to the local shopping centre to do taekwondo demonstrations to build membership. Kids from school would come by and see us. Like, can you imagine? Being fourteen and doing these demos in front of your friends? Mortifying.

Being sporty didn't help me fit in at school at all. Nup. Not at all. There were so many aerobics girls and ballerinas, and I was into full contact sports. I had friends at taekwondo, but they were all a little bit 'outcasty' too, and we all found solace in it. Our little taekwondo demonstration team was basically a very dynamic, active, glee club. We'd go to local primary schools and fêtes and perform to music, eat lunch in our trailer, it was like our little home. I kept doing it until I was 23, which is pretty embarrassing and way too old, but it just felt like I fitted in there.

Even in taekwondo, though, in competition, people would be like, 'Are you kidding? I'm gonna wipe the floor with her.' Mum would always put my hair in a scrunchie, and I'd have my blonde ponytail poking out of my helmet. Clearly I didn't fit into the competition world as a hardcore 'martial artist'. What I was, was academic and literary. I loved literature and philosophy and classics and I was always reading.

I always listened too much to what other people said. I always did what other people wanted. My Year 8 dance was a techno dance, not a formal, and Mum said that the 'biggest' thing to wear right then was a suit. She bought me a teal blazer with matching pants. All the girls, of course, wore dresses and miniskirts, and I was in this business suit, and not one boy asked me to dance. I was so embarrassed. I knew she was wrong all along, but I just didn't want to say, 'Hey, you know, this isn't right.'

Essentially, I was extremely socially awkward. I only hosted one sleepover and that was a very bad experience. I was always really organised, and that sort of spilled over into cleaning. Sometimes, if I couldn't deal with something, I'd clean. Mum would always yell at me because I'd just empty a drawer into the bin, which would make me feel better, but she'd have had important receipts or something in there.

So, for my 12th birthday, I asked for cleaning agents and some Ballerina cleaning cloths. When the girls came over for the sleepover, I said, 'Hey! Let's all clean the house!' Three of them were like '*Seriously?*' and they went off and amused themselves. But one girl was so sweet – she's still my friend today – and she helped. In the morning mum got up, and downstairs was spotless, the breakfast table was set, the napkins were folded ... and she said, 'What is *wrong* with you? I wanted mess! I wanted chaos! I wanted you to be tired and stay up all night!'

For me, though, most of the bullying and not fitting in happened at uni. Not many girls from school got in to uni, so I didn't know anybody. I was dating this boy and trying to fit in with his social clique – law and commerce students from the south side of town – and I was desperate to fit in with them. I changed the way I dressed, I cut my hair, I did everything I could think of. I tried so hard, but they were completely hung up on the fact I lived on the 'wrong' side of town. They kept saying, 'Where do you live? Close to the airport? Do you live on the runway?' I can't believe I wanted to make those people like me.

Sometimes I'd drive two hours to the other side of town and 'pop' into a party, as though I'd just driven by. They had mansions, the best cars, and the most amazing things, and for the first time in my life I felt embarrassed about where I'd grown up. I'd had the *best* upbringing, my parents were so generous, but for the first time I genuinely felt 'less than'.

A guy actually spat on me once. I couldn't surf, but I'd joined the surfing club just so I could go down to the beach with them and hang out. They made me the driver; I'd drive them all the way down to Bells Beach in my parents' Tarago, and they wouldn't talk to me and would go off surfing, then I'd drive them all the way back. This one guy hassled me about being a black belt; he wanted to see 'what I could do'. I explained that we don't do taekwondo on friends, and he decided I was 'full of shit', grabbed my throat, lifted me up against the wall, said I was a 'fake' and spat in my face. I did nothing. It was mortifying because I *had* a black belt. I was trained in the art of self-defence! I just couldn't ever use my voice, and say 'no', or tell people what I wanted. It's so important to use your voice when you're bullied. That's one regret I have; not smashing him, not showing him 'what I could do'.

When I was nineteen, I had a party and invited all those uni kids, and they didn't turn up. They didn't want to go on Citylink or leave South Yarra or something. Mum made pasta for everyone, big beautiful bowls of fantastic pasta, and we'd bought a little bit of alcohol, and we sat there waiting with my parents and they didn't show. I was so *deeply* embarrassed. At 9pm my dad rang some of my friends from taekwondo and an hour later they turned up. They weren't even really invited, but they turned up, and I remember my friend Brian coming in with beers on his shoulder like a real cool guy, and I could have just cried with the relief.

So I didn't have a 21st party. Too scarred! I haven't had a party since. Uni, for me, was just a disaster. It's always a disaster trying to be liked by people. I came out of uni with not one friend because I didn't stand up for myself.

It's only in the past decade or so that I've truly begun standing up for myself, saying 'no' to TV work so I can concentrate on writing fiction. And I've stepped away from fitness completely, to let my mind wander, to relax into imagining and daydreaming. When I'm stressed out I can't be creative – it's an absolute block. I've always loved reading, and now I prioritise it. I still get that nagging feeling I should be doing something else, but John Marsden once said you shouldn't write more than you read, and that's stuck with me. Finally, I'm not consumed with having to achieve things.

Being Angel on *Gladiator* seemed like a good idea. I was doing an internship at the *Herald Sun*, and I'd sent off submissions for a novel I'd written to agents and publishers – really putting myself out there – and never heard back. I'd had something like 75 rejections. Then I saw an ad in the paper for some TV stuff, and I thought, maybe if I was on TV, publishers would be more interested in my book?

The audition process was extremely gruelling. I thought I was auditioning to be a *competitor*, but at the end of like 100 burpees they went, 'You are Gladiator Angel!' and I was, 'What?' I hated it. I thought it was such a porno name. I wanted to be something strong and formidable, like 'Battleaxe'. Angel was a joke. I was so short, I'd walk into the arena and the competitors were like 'Pfft'. Once they put me in the air I was light and fast and ended up winning a lot, but, yeah, strength and power, not my strong point. But I realised early on, if I worked on TV only a little bit, I'd make enough money to pay rent and I could write as much as I wanted – four, five days a week.

As usual I worried that it wasn't the right move, and I told Mum I'd been offered a journalism job in Sydney. She said 'Excellent!' and bought me a brand new blazer, then I popped up on TV in a bra and panties and my parents were like, 'Oh. My. God.' It's something that I sort of regret, but then you just think, 'Hey, it's a bit of colour in my life. Meh, I was young and stupid.' Plus I met my fiancé doing *Gladiator*, so I guess it led to one good thing!

Because of being a Gladiator, I started doing self-defence courses in schools, and that put me in contact with a literary agent, but they just saw me as a Gladiator. And that's when I realised what I'd done. I thought it was a good plan, but you've got to choose your roles wisely. TV made it much more difficult for me to be respected as a writer.

I worked so hard on my fiction writing for so long, but I didn't tell anybody about it because it was never the right time. Then I came out with a book I'd been working on for years, and people were like 'Huh?' But, you know, I wouldn't change any of it, because it pushed me to hone my craft and really get better. I eventually sent off ten pages to a literary agency, and they signed me on the spot. The day I got my first publishing contract was the best day of my life.

Look, I think all my experiences were important, because I've learned resilience and patience and determination. I hang in there, which is vital if you work in publishing or TV. Rejection's a big part of it. Only this week I pitched two ideas for books and didn't get a reply. It's just part of the territory.

I see all the social disasters as character building. You really do realise the sorts of people you want as friends. It's actually not important that other people like you, but you do have to like yourself, and maybe I didn't like myself very much back then. I do now though, and I'm worth being a friend to anybody; I certainly don't put up with that crap anymore. I've really learned who *cares* if you don't fit in?

I embrace all the things I was embarrassed about and that I rejected: my parents in their uniforms, martial arts and the sign-written Tarago. What's important is they were passionate about something. I realise now that what they were saying, so loudly, was, 'It's okay to be different, and it's okay to be yourself.' All my experiences feed into my writing, into my books. My novels are 'ninja' novels, and all my characters are finding their voice and their confidence. They have a skill in their lives that no one can take away from them, and it's not about what they look like, or what other people think of them. That's very important. It's a full circle.

The empathy I have gained has absolutely fed into coaching. It's why I have something to offer kids who have been bullied, and why I'm really passionate about giving people the confidence to stand up for themselves. We go into schools and teach the kids some martial-arts moves, and they start really quietly, then get more confident, and then it's great to see them screaming and going, 'Hi-yah!'

It's also why, working on *The Biggest Loser*, I felt like I could understand. The contestants had been so ripped apart, so battered, by bullying, that they'd lost their self-worth. I know people looked at me and thought, 'As if you've ever experienced bullying or anything like it,' and I understand why. But at school I had the trifecta of braces, glasses and cystic acne – it was a whole different world back then.

I learned discipline from doing martial arts. That's a big one. Our house was very disciplined – the health-food thing, you know, no fast food, no soft drink. I remember going to a party once in junior school and being teased because I didn't know what a Redskin was.

I still love cleaning. It's more of a procrastination now. I find if I've got writer's block I'll start cleaning or vacuuming, and my fiancé knows if he comes home and the house is spotless, something's up. I find clarity through physically organising myself.

I wouldn't change anything. I think that it's all-important in developing character and empathising with other people. I'm still young, and I know what I want to do for the rest of my life, I'm secure in being the person I want to be, and I'm not worrying about working at Macca's. Not that there'd be anything wrong with that. Just be who you want to be and own it.

The greatest lesson you can learn in life is to be yourself and love your passion – and not worry about the end result but to live every day loving it. I read recently that we only have an average of 30,000 days on earth, and that seems so short to me. I feel as though I've wasted so many days worrying: about what other people thought of me, about what I should be doing. Worrying is anxiety about an imaginary future that usually never comes true.

EDDIE
PERFECT

For Edmund 'Eddie' Perfect, a restless, creative spirit, his years at a private school in a good suburb of Melbourne were about hiding in plain sight, keeping to himself, and trying not to suffocate from frustration and boredom. Hard to believe, but he was uncool, chubby, wussy, and artsy, entirely unsuited to a rigid school that valued fitness, fitting in, and traditional metrics of success. His career – as an actor, singer-songwriter, playwright, comedian, satirist and musical theatre composer – is an explosive push back against his school's expectations of compliance.

Ed's always looks for new challenges, guarding against being pigeon-holed, or favouring any one creative discipline. He's a Helpmann award-winning cabaret artist (for *Misanthropology*), and widely known as Mick Holland in Channel Ten's flagship comedy-drama *Offspring*. But he also wrote the scores for the Broadway musicals *Beetlejuice* and *King Kong*. He's been a host on *Play School*, a judge on *Australia's Got Talent*, a runner up on *The Masked Singer*, and written two plays which expose the hypocrisy of class – *The Beast* and *Vivid White* – oh, and a song cycle about the suburb he grew up in, Mentone.

This instinct to not be fenced in or contained can be directly traced back to high school, where every attempt was made to shove this arts-shaped boy into an engineering-shaped hole. Edmund Perfect (entirely his real name) loathed it all, and has sprinted in the opposite direction ever since.

I remember waiting high school out. Biding my time. I knew, as soon as it was over, I was going to get the hell out of there and do whatever I wanted. At our last assembly the school captain got up and did his speech, and said, 'You know they say that high school's the best years of your life,' and then he broke down and started sobbing. Really crying, really upset, saying, 'I can't believe we're going to leave all this behind. It's been so amazing.' I'm looking at him, astounded, thinking, 'Are you f**king kidding me? Anything and everything is going to be better than this.'

My school was an all-boys private one in Mentone down on the beach. It was a very disciplined place. You lined up, a bell went and you went here. Another bell went and you went there. I wasn't smoking pot behind the shed going, 'F**k the rules, man.' I was very much, 'I'm going to follow all the rules, and be diligent, and I'm going to play the model student,' but that doesn't mean I was happy with it. I definitely thought, 'This is ridiculously shit.'

It was clear that a certain kind of boy was going to be successful, and that that boy was not me. At my school it was all about becoming an engineer. Everyone wanted to be an engineer. I still don't even know what an engineer is, but lots of people wanted to be one. It was a cricket-in-the-summer, football-in-the-winter kind of place. The arts were not big there. At all. I mean you could *do* it, but it was never taken seriously. There was no music program, and the drama program was so small I didn't even study it.

Ironically our school motto was *Per Vias Rectas*, which when you're at an all-boys school sounds bad, but it means, 'By Right Paths'. And the way it was explained to us was there are right paths and there are wrong paths. You can choose your own path ... so long as it's engineering.

I was specifically told not to study the things I wanted to, because it wouldn't add up to a decent tertiary entrance score. I was determined to study the humanities whether it was beneficial to my grades or not, and I ended up getting the highest marks in my year, so they were wrong.

I mean, I was doing art in VCE, but I had teachers who, in a free period, would tell me off for working on my folio. In a free period! Telling you to do something serious! My recollection is of plotting and scheming, and *finding* time. I'm still like that. I don't like telling people what I'm up to.

My experience of high school was that it's a very constricted and narrow view of how people are supposed to be. It's particularly limiting and suburban. I was always creative, and wanted to be successful and do something unique, but none of that was ever recognised at school. It was kind of my own shameful little secret. I wanted to have a nose ring early on, and tattoos, and I bought garishly bright retro pants to wear. I'd never wear them now, but I had this need to express myself beyond the very limited means that were available.

I had a very strong inner life, and looking back I was clearly searching for a way to express myself, but I didn't have an avenue. I thought visual art was going to be it, you know, like, 'Here we go, it's something I'm good at it, I can do it on my own, you start with nothing and you create something.' And then I got into art school and discovered that I didn't have anything to say. I still really love visual art, and I can see what's good, but I'll never be good at it myself. It wasn't until I discovered songwriting, five or six years later, that I went, 'Oh, *this* is it.' I love words and music, and I've got ideas and I can express them.

I wasn't cool or popular at all. In the slightest. I was always chubby, even at primary school, and I was a fat kid all the way through high school. I wasn't massively overweight, more chubby, but it just diminishes your attractiveness. I wasn't good-looking either, so I was very much aware of my place. You don't hope for much.

I don't think I fitted in because, essentially, I was a bit of a wussbag. I was sensitive and I'd cry really easily. I wasn't tough, I didn't know how to stick up for myself, and in physical or verbal fights I had no skills. I wasn't confident, I was scared, and I was easily intimidated, which doesn't help. I was arty. I liked musical theatre. I did ballet when I was in primary school, and when someone found out about that, as you can imagine, it was pretty excruciating.

I was shithouse at sport. I mean I was okay at basketball but I was really bad at PE. We had a South-East Asian PE teacher, and his nickname for me was 'not so' which he thought was hilarious. Do you see what he did there? 'Not So Perfect'. There was a lot of canoeing on the beach. I remember falling out of the boat in really choppy waters on Port Phillip Bay, and him on a megaphone going, 'Get back in the boat, Not So, get back in the boat.' Ah, he hated my guts. I couldn't do a chin-up until I was maybe 25. I just used to dangle from the f**king monkey bars like a fat idiot.

You just get dismissed, really. It's pretty embarrassing. I can't remember ever being actively picked on about being bad at sport, just being overlooked and ignored. I was just never part of the mainstream. I had this sort of enemy, I don't know why, Patrick someone – I wish I could remember his name, he's a douchebag, that guy – who would for no reason just kind of grab me, twist my arm behind my back at lunchtime and slam my face into the locker. I was an occasional target for him, and I really hated it.

I wasn't at the bottom of the heap. I was *towards* the bottom, but there were people that were more bullied than me. I had friends, but I didn't ever like them particularly; they were allies I guess, but we had no shared interests. I found them increasingly embarrassing and stifling – there was an alpha male in the group I didn't get on with – and I thought the whole hierarchy thing was ridiculous.

As I got towards Years 11 and 12 I extricated myself from them, to pretty much no one. It wasn't an unhappy withdrawal, I didn't feel lonely. I spent most of my lunchtimes in the art room working on my folio rather than having to deal with hanging out in the schoolyard and that dynamic.

I got on really well with adults, and I had good art, history and literature teachers, so I threw myself into the work. The bonus was I learned to love the learning, and the teachers that liked me encouraged me. My literature teacher gave me a card at the end of Year 12 with the Robert Frost poem, 'The Road Not Taken'. When I read that it was freaking mind-blowing. It was exactly how I felt.

If I think about it, most of my formative events were being rejected by girls that I liked, and being really hurt by that. It happened every time. I had the hots for this girl, Zoe, and I got up the courage to ask her to my Year 12 formal. And when we got there, within five minutes, she was getting it on with my archenemy Patrick. That sort of thing happened a lot.

I had sisters, so I was really good at talking to girls, and not good at exploiting them, which is 99 per cent of how you get by with girls at high school. I didn't feel right about taking advantage, so I'd always, eventually, become their friends. Or we'd be friends first and it would never become anything else because they value your friendship. You know. One of those guys.

Our school finally had a musical, and I got into that in Year 11. It was amazing because I got to meet girls doing something I was actually good at. That changed everything. I was making a kind of headway during that process. Until one day. I used to ride my bike home past the bus stop where all the girls from the local schools converged. There would be at least two hundred girls there every afternoon, and it was the most hideously self-conscious stretch of road I'd ride along. To them I was just some twat in a blazer, they wouldn't have looked twice, but I always felt like 200 pairs of eyes were on me.

Then one time, after the musical, I was riding home with my helmet on the handlebars – because it wasn't cool to wear a helmet – and I thought I'd ride without my hands on the handlebars. So I'm cycling no-hands-no-helmet past this bus stop, and then, like a miracle, this girl yells out, 'Hey, Eddie!' I'm like, 'Is this possible?' And it's a pretty, popular girl from the musical waving at me, so I kind of turned around, waved, and rode into the back of a parked car.

I didn't even break my fall with my hands. I smashed my face into the back windscreen, the bike crumpled in half, I hit the deck, and 200 girls just pissed themselves laughing. And you know when you're hurt but you pretend that you're not, and you leap up really quickly and pretend that it's all okay? Well, I leapt up straight away, but I was in agony, because those gears that are kind of like bunny ears, one of them had stabbed me right in the scrotum, I'd hurt my leg so much that I couldn't put my weight on it, and I'd actually cracked the windscreen with my face. And I couldn't ride away because the frame was buckled, so I had to pick up my bike and limp away from 200 laughing girls. Yeah. So that undid all the good work I'd done. It was like, 'I've got to move towns. Now.'

What motivated me a lot, and probably still motivates me, was getting out. I hated Mentone. Really hated it. I hated food courts, and tenpin bowling alleys, and that whole community vibe. My dad was a school teacher, and well-liked, so we were very much a part of the 'community' – people knowing what's going on, and keeping tabs on you, and all that kind of stuff. I wanted to find my own community. I was working at an education bookstore during the holidays, stacking shelves, and thinking, 'I've got to get away from this.'

Shane Warne: The Musical was the first thing I did, finally, accidentally, that Mentone would be vaguely interested in. I got asked to sing the National Anthem for the Boxing Day tests, and the effect that had on people from Mentone was full-on. Like all of a sudden I'd somehow combined all of my artistic wankery with sport, and it blew people's minds – people were ringing up my family in tears. It was the pinnacle of success to them.

It was kind of a funny moment, but it also made me realise I don't give a shit. From school I was originally motivated by, 'I'll be a success, and I'll stick it up all of you and show you,' but now I don't care. I don't do it for that reason at all any more. But everyone's motivated by something, and if you're lucky – and I consider myself lucky – you find a medium that you really love and are genuinely interested in.

The other motivation was girls. I wasn't good-looking enough, or sporty enough, to fit in, and I realised that if I wanted to get anywhere with girls I'd need to develop some skills. I was also going to use my skills to get out, and not in a noisy way. I was never arrogant. I just knew I was going to do my own thing and one day it would work out.

One flow-on from school, because the dreams I had weren't considered aspirational, is that I've got an almost pathological fear of talking about my projects with other people. Letting people know somehow seems to diminish it. You know how people are curious about what other people think about them? I'm terrified. I will do everything to avoid finding out what people think about me, because I've built up such a strong thing about not giving a shit. That protects me, but it also doesn't invite in any possible nice things. I don't even really know what my friends think about me, and as soon as people start talking about me I get really uncomfortable.

I think the institution of high school is, at its core, about early detection. It worries me. I think high school is getting so career-focused. They want to form you and then send you off in a particular direction. I resisted that entirely, and I resisted it by just shutting the hell up. But what I've learned from that is I listen to my gut. I go, 'This feels right,' or 'This doesn't feel right.' I don't make a song and dance about it but I extricate myself when it's not me. I don't pledge allegiance to anyone, because I feel constrained when I'm with just one group of people. I really love doing comedy, and it's given me the most opportunities out of any industry I've worked in, but I don't say 'I'm a comedian' and just live in that world.

I like to be able to do stuff, and I don't like people telling me I can't. I'm very sensitive to criticism or even the slightest comment – I fear even just listening. How does any one person know what another person's potential could be? Even in general conversation, people can shape your mind and the way you think about yourself and your possibilities.

It happens a lot, even the people you love the most can damage you with a very narrow view of what you're capable of doing. People are really worried about what others think of them, and that probably holds them back more than anything else. My way of getting around that has been avoiding people's opinions. Or just telling them, 'F**k you, I'm going to do it anyway.'

I've got no qualifications to write music, I've got no qualifications to write scripts, or even do comedy. I found all of it terrifying, but I made myself do it, because I thought I *might* be able to do it. And I meet *heaps* of people who go, 'Oh I'm not a writer,' or 'I'm not a songwriter,' and I don't know why they made that decision. I don't have any right to call myself anything, except I've done it a lot, and now it's just accepted.

I feel sick going back to my high school. It's a weird place. It's not traumatic and it's not painful, it's just so uninteresting. It's just ... bleugh. You know The Nothing in *The Neverending Story*? It was like this beige, indescribable cardigan coming for you, and if you're not able to run away and escape it, it's going to envelop you, and you're going to become beige like everybody else.

So you've just gotta run. And put your fingers in your ears, and go 'Lalalalala', and do what you want, and not worry about what other people think. It might make me seem detached or aloof or difficult to know, but it's certainly helped me do what I wanted to do. Later on you work out that school is such a tiny part of life. It can be really great for some people, or it can be really horrific, but even the worst things, like riding into a parked car, can actually become funny.

And you're not going to remain that person. When I was in Year 12, I saw a piece of pottery in the window of the school library, this really shit ceramic pot, saying 'Eddie Perfect Year 7', and I never could remember making that pot. Obviously I must have, but we're all a bit like that f**ked-up pot – once you leave, you're not the person you were in high school anymore.

School's the best catch-all system they can churn people through. Some people will get bumped or squashed, and not everyone's going to come out perfectly. But once you get out you can do whatever you like. That's why I find it hard to talk about school. I kind of don't want to acknowledge the past at all, because I prefer to diminish it and take its power away. I draw a line, like, 'Done. Whatever. Move forward.'

I shall be telling this with a sigh
Somewhere ages and ages hence:
Two roads diverged in a wood, and I,
I took the one less traveled by,
And that has made all the difference.

From 'The Road Not Taken' by Robert Frost

RESOURCES

Headspace

Headspace supports young people aged 12 to 25 with general health, mental health and well-being, alcohol and other drugs and education, employment and other services. To find your nearest headspace centre or for online and telephone mental health support visit the Headspace website.

headspace.org.au

Kids Helpline

Kids Helpline is Australia's only free telephone and online counselling service specifically for children and young people aged between five and 25. Kids Helpline is there any time for any reason, no matter how big or small. We are there whenever a young person needs us, 24/7. We care. We Listen. Any time and for any reason.

1800 55 1800

kidshelp.com.au

Reach Out Australia

ReachOut.com is an online mental-health service to help young people through tough times. Combining fact sheets, stories, apps and forums, ReachOut.com is the help young people need, where and when they need it.

au.reachout.com

ACKNOWLEDGEMENTS

Firstly, as is proper, particularly in a book about transcending bullying, disrespect and hardship, I acknowledge that I live and work on unceded land. Naarm, or Melbourne, is part of the traditional lands of the Kulin nation, and I pay my respects to the Wurundjeri and Boonwurrung peoples, and to Elders past and present.

This book is the work of many hands, as all books are. Every book creates a community, and requires untold generosity and support from all involved. *Hard Knocks* is in your hands because people believe in it, and I am grateful. Like many who battled their way through their school years, I still harbour a chip of loneliness at my core, and it is a wonderful and nourishing thing to be believed in.

First and foremost, deep gratitude to the people I interviewed for *Hard Knocks*, who gave me their time, the gift of trust and their stories. Any errors are mine, not theirs. Everyone was so open and fierce about sharing their experiences and what they've learned, wanting to offer reassurance, inspiration and perspective. It takes a lot to expose your vulnerabilities and how you were shaped and made, and they did it because they care, and because they know what it's like. It's been an honour, and every story here has torn my heart in one way or another. There is much courage captured within these pages. Thank you.

Thank you to Affirm Press, in particular Martin Hughes and Keiran Rogers. Affirm's ethos is to do good in the world, and I am proud to be on board that train. *Hard Knocks* is the third iteration of a concept which began with *Don't Peak at High School* in 2011, and it is rare to be given this degree of commitment.

I absolutely acknowledge the patience and kindness of the editing team at Affirm, who shepherded me through a pandemic. It was a challenging time. So, thank you to Kevin O'Brien, Coco McGrath, Natasha Seymour – and Armelle Davies for copyediting *Hard Knocks*, and sitting on my shoulder like a wise owl bringing her objectivity and craft.

A big thank you, also, to the interns at Affirm who worked on the interview transcriptions for me. Transcribing, and its associated checking for accuracy, is the very definition of a thankless task – so, thank you to Austin Ceravolo, Madeleine Corbel, Alistair Trapnell, Kate Fleming and Banpreet Shahi.

Finally, the most gratitude to my partner, Greg, who not only lived in close quarters with me for the longest lockdowns in the world, but staunchly supported me, and during the writing of *Hard Knocks* kept me fed, watered, and turned towards the light. Thank you, honey.